ON THE ROAD TO TIBET

AN EPIC JOURNEY THROUGH WESTERN CHINA IN 1910

FRANK KINGDON-WARD

On the Road to Tibet

By Frank Kingdon-Ward

With a new Preface by Graham Earnshaw

Spellings have largely been left as in the original

ISBN-13: 978-988-8769-14-8

© 2021 Earnshaw Books Ltd

HISTORY / Asia / China

EB153

All rights reserved. No part of this book may be reproduced in material form, by any means, whether graphic, electronic, mechanical or other, including photocopying or information storage, in whole or in part. May not be used to prepare other publications without written permission from the publisher except in the case of brief quotations embodied in critical articles or reviews. For information contact info@earnshawbooks.com

Published by Earnshaw Books Ltd. (Hong Kong)

Preface

FRANK KINGDON-WARD was a dedicated explorer, addicted to the great vastness of western China, Central Asia and the wonders of Tibet. He was a plant collector, but that was, it seems to me, an excuse for what he really liked to do, which was to travel through the wilds of that part of the world which is so physically magnificent, so central to the past of the human race, and so laced with cultures and traditions that had depth and meaning beyond anything else in the world.

The east Himalayas was his primary area of operation—a region of high plains, dramatic mountains, deep gorges and rushing rivers. Human beings were scarce, but the richness of plant life more than made up for it, and over the decades Kingdon-Ward traversed the region more than anyone before, or probably since. From the provinces of Shaanxi and Gansu, then south to Burma and northeast India, he was tracing the outlines of eastern Tibet. And he delved into that region more than once, starting with the expedition narrated in this book, *On the Road to Tibet*.

Kingdon-Ward was passionately attached to travel through these remote places, and to his task of collecting specimens of life there. *On The Road to Tibet* talks more about the collection of animal specimens than plants, to the extent that either are mentioned at all, but he was, at the time, still young and finding his way. His starting point was the approach of the Anglo-Saxon traveler of the 19th Century, which typically involved a gun and the gathering of carcasses. But he transcended it.

ON THE ROAD TO TIBET

Kingdon-Ward was born in 1885 in Manchester. His father was a botanist who became Professor of Botany at Cambridge university, and Kingdon-Ward himself went to Christ's College, at Cambridge in 1904, and graduated in Natural Sciences Tripos, a collection of subjects covering the natural world. He then immediately departed in 1907 for China, to take up a post as schoolteacher at the Shanghai Public School, a school run by the British-dominated Shanghai Municipal Council for foreign children in the International Settlement. On his way there, his ship stopped at Singapore, and Kingdon-Ward took the opportunity to briefly experience a tropical forest. "I just wanted to steep myself in an atmosphere, to revel in the scents, and to see with my own eyes all the exuberance of life that the warmth, humidity, and equinoctial time-sequence of the tropics produces." That desire to immerse himself in raw nature never left him.

The school teaching job was merely an excuse to be in East Asia, and to prepare for his chosen role as a collector of plant and other specimens. Only two years after arriving in Shanghai, he started out on a major expedition, the first of twenty five that spanned half a century, until his death in 1958 at the age of seventy-two. In September 1909, he attached himself to an American zoological expedition to western China. His companions were more interested in killing animals, but he did collect some plant samples which he donated to the Botany School at Cambridge.

His later adventures traveling through the lands to the east and north of the Himalayas belong in another place, and almost suffice it to say that Kingdon-Ward became one of the great plant collectors of all time, and wrote a number of books documenting his travels and discoveries, including *The Land of the Blue Poppy* and *Plant Hunting on the Edge of the World*. He was in Burma when the Japanese attacked after Pearl Harbor, and used his extensive

PREFACE

knowledge of the region to escape through to India. After the war, he used his skills to help the U.S. military search for lost aircrews.

Kingdon-Ward clearly had deep wells of endurance and persistence, and his eye for detail was just in the process of being trained in the story told in this book. But his descriptions of scenes and situations, and his understanding of what he was witnessing, placed him even then towards the quality end of travel writing. His comments in places reflect the deep self-confidence of Anglo-Saxons in that pre-WWI era, but he caveats his arrogance enough times that you know he is thinking it through in a way that many other members of the white "master race," as it then in many ways was, did not.

What emerges most from his narrative is his love of nature, his curiosity about all things, both natural and human, and eagerness to engage with the unknown. He was a pure adventurer.

The trip documented here took just seventeen days short of a year, from Shanghai and back to Shanghai. Following such a trip from a century and more ago on a modern-day map is usually not easy. The place names have mostly changed—sometimes just the spelling, from Wade-Giles to pinyin, but more often the actual names of places have changed as well. But in this case, it is possible to discern pretty clearly the route that Kingdon-Ward and his friends took.

The party first went up the Yangtze to the Han River, one of the key tributaries of that waterway, which enters the great flow just above today's Wuhan, in the center of central China plain. Up the Han to Xiangyang and then over the mountains to the north, into the great valley of the Yellow River, to the town of Huayin, to the east of Xi'an. They ascended Huashan, one of the holiest of China's mountains, and then traveled on westwards to Xi'an, stopping on the way at the Huaqing springs where the

ON THE ROAD TO TIBET

Empress Dowager had stayed in 1900 during the Boxer Rebellion and where, twenty-six years later, Chiang Kai-shek would be held hostage.

On leaving Xi'an, they headed southwest to the city of Hanzhong, in southern Shaanxi Province, close to the border with Sichuan, then continued northwest into southern Gansu. They traveled to Choni, the Tibetan name for a region of today's southern Gansu province, then went south through other Tibetan areas before circling back, south and east to Chengdu. After a sojourn there, they headed southwest back into the mountains, before retreating to Emei Shan, even then a tourist destination, it seems. And from there, by junk to Chungking and on eastwards back along the Yangtze River to Shanghai.

Kingdon-Ward on several occasions displays both his deep interest in vegetation and ability to describe sights encountered on his travels, which unpinned so much of his life's work in the decades to come. Here is a rosy example from *On The Road to Tibet*:

> "Autumn in the mountains of western China is glorious. Between the fierce heat of the summer, when all vegetation is parched and gasping, and winter with its dreadful monotony of limitless snow, withered grass, and naked trees, come three months of radiant days and crisp nights. Then the flowers bloom as though spring had come again; the faded vegetation, at dawn dripping with dew or sparkling with the first frost, turns many-colored; persimmon trees laden with golden fruit deck the mountain slopes with spots of fire; and at night the moon, climbing up the sky, presently licks the tops of the black mountains and sends shafts of light down into the shadowy valley,

PREFACE

where it glances on the white granite pebbles of the river bed and illuminates the rapids with streaks of dancing silver."

Religion is in various ways a regular theme of the book, both because of contacts on the trip with Christian missionaries in multiple places, but also prompted by visits to Buddhist temples, and Kingdon-Ward has strong views on the subject. Taoism, at least in his era and in his view, was nothing more than a "grotesque philosophy" and Buddhism was weak and corrupted and on the wane.

"Buddhism was introduced from India during the first century, and has been so mutilated since that there are really no Buddhists left in China. Those who periodically visit the Buddhist temples and toss their cash to the sharks waiting to snap them up, go there to ask for rain or riches, sunshine or health, and are no more Buddhists than are those persons who pay perfunctory visits to church, Christians."

And what of the future of Christianity in China? Kingdon-Ward is not optimistic, but does say that the main legacy of Christianity would be in the areas of education and medical care. And indeed that turned out to be the case, at least in terms of the impact of the religion up to the end of the 20th century. So many of the major hospitals and schools in major cities were set up by foreign missionaries. In terms of Tibetan Buddhism and the large number of Buddhist priests—lamas—is damning: he describes them as debauched ecclesiastics. "The passing of Buddhism may take generations, but the hand-writing is on the wall," he concludes.

Opium is another constant topic in such travel books of that era, and while Kingdon-Ward makes the case that China is at least complicit in the crime of mass opium addiction, he does, with what appears to be reluctance, put the main share of blame at the feet of the "old country" — England. But he does report significant progress in the extermination of opium cultivation in regions they passed through, including Sichuan. "During more than three months spent in this province, during which time we traveled hundreds of miles, we did not see a single opium poppy," he writes.

He also addresses the question of the arrogance of foreigners in an era when China was viewed as being a hopeless case, and refers to people who abused the special status foreigners had in China. It's a phenomenon which is not unknown even today, but there is still a touch of the "Out of my way, I'm British" attitude in what he says:

"We heard a good deal of gossip from time to time about the ill-treatment of natives by foreigners, and unfortunately we know that some of the incidents referred to were only too true. Men have openly boasted that they have traveled half across the country without disbursing a single cash, and others have earned an ugly reputation for emphasizing their orders by the display of, or the theatrical suggestion of, physical violence. In dealing with Chinese as in dealing with any other un-educated people, especially Asiatics, it is sometimes necessary to employ force, if you mean to have your own way; but there are ways and means and degrees of applying it, differing in men and beasts. Certain Americans, Germans, Frenchmen, even Britons on occasion, have left an indelible and despicable impression among the natives."

Finally with great prescience, he accurately predicts the future Chengdu: "So we leave Chengtu, the coming city of the west, not without a hope registered that the oft discussed, and already initiated railway, will one day bring it within easy reach of [the river town of] I-chang, and the great highway of China."

Kingdon-Ward died in 1958, at what today would be

PREFACE

considered the too-young age of seventy-three. But he left a rich record behind him, of which this book is a key part.

Graham Earnshaw
November 2021

ON THE ROAD TO TIBET

ON THE ROAD TO TIBET

BY
FRANK KINGDON-WARD

———◆———

REPRINTED FROM A SERIES OF ARTICLES IN THE
"SHANGHAI MERCURY."

1

The Junk Voyage

On the evening of 5th October, after an uneventful voyage of six hundred miles up the Yang-tze, we gathered on the junk at the mouth of the Han river, ready for an early start on the morrow.

With daybreak came the whining of ropes through the blocks, a raw autumn morning with a silver half moon overhead and an orange glow over against the black city to the east; out of the river mist stood the huge smoking chimneys of the Han-yang steel works, set like long smudges against the dawn, and as the sail began to fill and the current to bubble noisily against our bows, came the hoot and roar of the sirens, calling to work.

And thus as the sun rose, we sailed out into the wide free world.

Junk life on the lower Han river is tedious, for the country is quite flat throughout, the high mud banks, lined almost continuously with villages, obscuring only a monotonous expanse of buck-wheat, cotton and millet fields, while a faint blue line waved across the horizon indicates the distant hills.

When the wind was favourable we sailed, but it never is favourable for any length of time, on account of the huge serpentine bends which the river takes, sweeping as it does round three parts of a circle, to turn abruptly on itself and twist the other way.

ON THE ROAD TO TIBET

When not sailing we tracked, with four or five men on the tow-line, and under these conditions thirty miles was a good day's journey.

Progress however, if not breathless, was steady for several days, and then came disaster.

The heavens were opened, down came the rain, and for three days the cloud canopy dripped mercilessly upon us. To sail was impossible, for there was no wind; to track was out of the question, for the banks gave no foothold. Central and Western China had been very hardly handled by the unprecedented rains of early autumn, and in many parts of Hupeh, Honan and Shensi roads were impassable, river banks bursting, crops ruined, and food at famine prices.

Nor were signs of disaster lacking on the Han, a gigantic breach in the bank, fully four hundred yards across, shortly coming into view, and the country being thereby converted into a lake as far as the eye could reach. Out of the water tree tops alone stood up like fretted islands, and the people said that it was possible to get across country to Ichang by boat.

Several thousand persons had recently lost their lives in this catastrophe, and how many acres of crops had been destroyed it would be difficult to estimate.

From this point onwards we found the banks ripped bare of vegetation often over a distance of a mile from the present limits of the water, and the land plastered with sand and mud. Here thousands of geese, duck and occasionally bustard, made their feeding ground, and shooting them proved a welcome diversion to the day's routine and added variety to the larder.

The next delay was caused by wind.

For some days the crew had been whistling for a wind without result, but they whistled once too often, and it came with a rush in the middle of the night, a chilly blast from the west, and again for three days we were unable to move. During the enforced halt we visited Nganlin-fu, but it is an uninteresting place. The missionaries told us sadly that here the seed fell on but stony ground, and if the people were anything like as stony-hearted as the city appeared stony-broke we could well believe it.

In addition to agriculture the chief occupations of the riparian population were fishing and washing for gold.

Men would stand on the bank day and night, slowly sweeping a hand-net through the murky water with monotonous regularity; or they would stand up in a boat and sling a drag net overboard at a fish, with the skill of a retarius; or they would let down into the water a great square-framed net pivoted on an upright support in the bows of the boat, and wait for a fish to sit in it; or they would move up and down the reaches with half a dozen cormorants sitting on the edge of the boat, prospecting for a bite and looking very wise.

There were other ways of doing it too, and they all seemed equally unable to entice fish ashore except the men with the shrimping nets, who were the most unsuccessful of all; for though we saw hundreds engaged in this placid task, we never saw a fish the worse for it.

Their only competitors were the herons, but I should have preferred to be a heron for choice.

However someone must have been catching fish, since we were able to purchase it.

Washing the sand for gold was another precarious method of earning a livelihood, for the Han is no river of golden sand. The auriferous layers are generally a few feet below the surface, and the sand is carried to the river side to be panned in a primitive manner.

By this method, five men would extract on the average about three-hundredths of an ounce of gold a day, which would bring them in two hundred cash, or a penny a day per man.

Should the venture prove much more lucrative, however, they would soon quit; it is only because as gold seekers they earn no more than the coolie they can pursue their peaceful calling uninterrupted.

On 26th October we reached Fentschong, a considerable market town which stands opposite to the prefectural city of Hsiang-yang. These two cities, in those days connected by a bridge across the Han river, were besieged by the Mongol General Kublai Kahn for four years (1268-1271) and it was not till he had obtained cannon from Persia, where his brother reigned as Shah, that they were reduced.

It was probably not a very Trojan defence however, nor a Homeric investment either.

Just above Hsian-yang are a few low hills, one of which is capped by an unpretentious Buddhist temple.

But the Franciscan monks have outbid Buddha.

True to their policy of hitting the Chinaman right in the eye by an appeal to his gross materialistic instincts, they have erected a colossal cross on the topmost hill, which being nearer to heaven than the Buddhist temple, must be more worth striving after, and the convert may imagine himself to be dwelling in the shadow of Calvary itself.

The lao-pan made trouble at Fentschong, because he had come to the end of his money.

The unbusiness-like custom prevails in Chinese junking circles of losing on the up trip, which in the case of a journey from Hankow to Lao-ho-kow, takes about four weeks and costs about thirty taels — hardly sufficient to feed the crew for a month, and making money on the down trip, which takes six or eight days and costs some fifty taels, besides which the boat will take down a heavy cargo from the interior.

THE JUNK VOYAGE

According to the immemorial custom of China, the lao-pan had been paid before starting, with the exception of a small sum which was kept back in order to retain some hold over him in addition to the signed contract.

By the terms of this latter, he was to receive 28,000 cash at Hankow, 4,000 at Scha-yang (about half way), and 4,000 more at Lao-ho-kow — thirty taels, or about £3 15s. in all.

But his next windfall must have been already mortgaged up to the hilt some time before, and having bought some stores for the crew, he left Hankow without a cash. At Fen-tschong he had already spent his next installment of 4,000 cash, and the balance was not due till we reached Lao-ho-kow.

As the lao-pan was in straits once more, he used every ingenious argument to make us pay up the last 4,000 cash at once.

The old man vowed he could not feed his crew unless he had the money; that he wanted to feed them well, so that they could work hard; that rice was cheap here, and that if he got in all his stores now it would save future delays; and, finally, that he had no intention of breaking through the signed contract, but that he would regard the advance as a loan only, to be repaid at Lao-ho-kow by — not asking for any more!

So harrowing was his story that we at last gave in, though we now had no hold over him except the signed contract. This, however, on the lao-pan's side was never abused, and I may say at once that when John Chinaman makes a promise, and signs a contract, he keeps it; at least that was our experience.

Even this however was not enough to satisfy the rapacious old scoundrel, for he quietly proceeded to pawn his daughter's bracelet, and finished up by borrowing money from a friend ashore.

Our cook got into difficulties at Fen-tschong too, but extricated himself rather neatly.

Having gone ashore marketing, he left his basket, with a few purchases and some packets of money in the shop while he went elsewhere — a thing done every where in China.

However when he returned a packet containing 700 cash was missing, and the shopkeeper was of course blissfully ignorant.

The cook therefore told him that he would have to come down to the boat, if he wanted to be paid, and the unsuspecting shop-keeper came, and was paid, minus 700 cash.

A fine rhetorical effort, lurid, if somewhat irrelevant, greeted this sally, but it was hardly sincere. Above Hsian-yang a splendid causeway has been built for upwards of a mile, to keep the river within bounds. It is a pity that such public works, which are sorely needed, are not more frequently put up.

A filibustering expedition was responsible for an amusing episode one night, when, having reached a part of the country suffering from the effects of the famine, and inclined to be lawless, we tied up close to a police boat.

Away out in the night we were awakened by the shouting of men, the banging of the gongs, and the explosion of firearms; the village had been attacked.

The little official jumped ashore from the police junk only half dressed, forgetting in his distress to take his gun, for which he presently hastened back.

Then he flung himself madly into the fray, whooping like an Indian brave on the warpath, and firing off his blunderbus right and left in the most lunatic fashion.

"I'll have you yet, I'll have you yet," he yelled, and it certainly seemed as though he would, for having run up against a man circling round an orbit which crossed that of his own meteoric progress, he gave him such a bad time that the poor fellow was forced to confess that he was really only one of the official's own men mistaken in the dark for a brigand.

THE JUNK VOYAGE

At length the noise subsided, the official returned rather crestfallen, saying that he could not follow the thieves (but adding that he would have them yet), and we got to sleep again.

It turned out to have been a very puny affair really, in spite of the racket, an affair of almost nightly occurrence. There were no casualties.

A day or two later we met the late Taotai of one of the up river cities coming down; he had resigned his post, which probably means that he had accepted a more lucrative one. It was a regular water carnival. First came a police boat, gay with flags, manned by eight or ten policemen in gaudy red tunics, these amphibians having turned into bargees for the time being; then came junks with the great man's furniture sticking out of the windows, piled on the deck, or tied to the mast; junks with his wives — also sticking out of the windows; junks with his children, and junks with his accessory relatives down to the third and fourth generation.

Finally came the great man himself surrounded by several more police boats, and followed by a hustle of small boats, like threshers following a whale, all eager to pick up anything which the procession dropped overboard.

There was quite a fleet, thirty or forty boats of all sizes, decorated with flags and trappings. It was like the Spanish Armada.

The terrible confusion of weights and measures is soon remarked by every traveller in the interior.

"How far distant is Lao-ho-kow?" we asked the crew at 2 p.m. on the last day.

"Forty li," the lao-pan replied.

An hour later the question was repeated.

"Eighty li," came the unblushing answer.

It was the same in the mountains; we would start off before dawn on an eighty li tramp and arrive hot and dusty at a wayside inn, to learn, over a bowl of maize meal soup or a basin of mien, that we had come thirty li; it was heartbreaking, but we would reach our destination at four o'clock just the same.

" How far is it to Chi-t'ow-kuan?" we asked at Luan-chang, when arranging the next day's stage.

"Seventy li," volunteers a youngster.

"Eighty!" reply the old ones, shaking their heads.

"A little over sixty," the muleteers tell us.

Arrived at Chi-t'ow-kuan," how far is it to Luan-chang," we ask.

"Eighty li!" they all agree, without hesitation.

Every man is his own foot-rule, and hence it soon becomes a mere rule of thumb.

Again, not only does the number of cash that will exchange for one tael of silver vary in different localities, and fluctuate daily in the same place, but the weight of the tael itself (which may be regarded as equivalent to our ounce), varies greatly.

Furthermore, though two cities may happen to possess a similar ounce, each will have its own idea of how many ounces go to a catty, and catties to a picul.

Thus at Lao-ho-kow there were twenty-four pounds to the bushel (to put it into English measure), while at Kin-tsi-kuan the number had risen to forty-eight. But it surpasses human ingenuity when the number of ounces to the pound varies with the article purchased, as was the case at Fen-ts-chong.

When purchasing meat there were twenty ounces in a pound, but with sugar we could only find sixteen of them, and when we came to salt, the number had fallen to twelve, which added a rather disturbing element of uncertainty to marketing.

It is annoying, too, to reach a place where a hundred cash is

THE JUNK VOYAGE

really only eighty; in fact you don't quite understand what this means until, after haggling over the price of a thing for half an hour and eventually closing with the man for a thousand cash (to your secret satisfaction), you find that you still have to pay twelve hundred for it (to your intense mortification).

The only plan in a place like that is to sell things instead of buying them.

But the most insidious case of exchange we met with at Lao-ho-kow, where the telegraph office was giving 1,400 cash to the tael, while at the same time the post office would only give 1,300.

Pushing the thing to its logical conclusion, we actually found the following paradox stalking in broad daylight. Though there were more cash to the tael in a city A, than in a city B (that is cash was worth less at the former) yet with a thousand cash you could buy more rice at A than you could at B because there happened also to be more pounds to the bushel there?

It would throw a chartered accountant off his balance in a week, though the missionaries have to grapple with the chaos.

On the night of 28th October we reached Lao-ho-kow, a mud-walled city of little interest, four hundred and twenty miles above Hankow; and here we had to transfer to a much smaller boat for the voyage up the shallows and rapids of the Tan river.

So far we had revelled in a palatial junk drawing a foot of water, but now we were forced to put up with a pao-chwan, a low, mat-roofed stern-sweeper, drawing only eight inches. However, the population had thinned out considerably; the number of people crowded into that fifty foot junk would have made a sanitary inspector blanch.

Amidships were Their Excellencies and the cook, rats and black beetles skilfully interlarding themselves into all intermediate standing room, and frequently in the night encroaching over the frontiers.

The crew, four in number, concealed themselves forward, under the fo'csle deck-boards, and quartered in the after deck house were the remainder, namely, the lao-pan and his wife, and his son, and his son's wife, and his son's wife's baby, and an obscure relative and her child, and a friend.

The baby wasn't a bit obscure — she was one of the most obvious articles in the boat, but the poor little thing was sick most of the time.

On moonlight evenings, when the junk was tied up for the night, and the baby girl had gone off into a feverish sleep, it was the strangest thing in the world to sit on deck and listen to the old lao-pan calling gently to her soul to come back, come back, before it flew too far away; when sick children fall asleep, their souls leave their bodies and wander abroad into the night. "Hwei-lai! hwei-lai!" (come back!) he chanted, looking up to the brilliant stars.

"Hwei-lai-liao! hwei-lai-liao!" (I have come back!) crowed the aged grandmother in reply, taking the part of the baby soul.

It was a pretty thin disguise, but it seemed to comfort the old man, and so the picturesque pantomime went on night after night till the baby was well again.

Superstition's skinny finger digs us all in the ribs; it is only a matter of degree. Certainly the Chinese are a very superstitious race, but it is the superstition of custom, the dead ritual of a hoary tradition, rather than the superstition of ignorance. On the other hand their spell-bound conservatism has lost nothing through the ages except the sap of life which once quickened those rites where-of only the fleshless skeletons now remain.

Now the superstition of ignorance consists in attributing indefinite effects to definite causes, there being no relation between the two either in magnitude or direction, and not necessarily even in sequence; if one is sufficiently superstitious, effects may be considered to precede their causes.

The result is that markedly superstitious people are as fidgety as if they were sitting on a barrel of gunpowder during a pyrotechnic display.

But the Chinaman is not fidgety; he is the most imperturbable person in the world. Certainly he does not attribute indefinite effects to definite causes; he generally looks after the causes and leaves the effects to look after themselves.

He doesn't believe it at all; he only does it. That is the superstition of custom.

One day we met a man emerging from an inn with a bundle of incense, and on asking him where he was going and what he was going to do, Dr. Smith received the following reply:

"My little daughter has fits, and I am going to burn incense to the gods, that they may cure her."

"But your gods are made of wood and mud aren't they?" and when the old man had admitted that it was so:

"Well then, how can a lump of mud cure your daughter of fits? And yet you spend your money on incense, to burn in front of a lifeless bit of gaudy mud!"

That puzzled the old man; he couldn't explain it at all, and seemed surprised that he had never thought of it himself, though he quite agreed that it was so.

"But if you prayed to the one true God, He might listen to you and cure your daughter," he was told.

"Yes, that's right, the foreign excellency is right," broke in the innkeeper patronisingly," pray to the Heavenly Grandfather!"

"Ask and ye shall receive" is the fundamental doctrine of Christianity, but its intense vagueness corresponds well with our definition of superstition.

Besides I've tried it, and it doesn't always work. I remember one summer afternoon when I was a small boy asking most fervently for a pop-gun to frighten the birds with.

After waiting what seemed to a little boy playing in a big country garden an epoch, I got half the apparatus — the cork part; but the rest of the outfit never came along at all.

The Chinaman on the other hand is commendably explicit, and he spends any amount of time and money bribing the gods to dole out material benefits open handedly, a course of action which has only the objection above hinted at — that the results are rarely commensurate with the effort expended.

He asks this god for rain, that god for riches, a third for health, and the fact that he doesn't get any of them is sufficient to warrant his continuing to ask.

If I upset the salt, I believe that dire but unspecified evil will follow, sooner or later; if I remember to throw a pinch over my left shoulder, the panic subsides, for I know that some subtle influence will instantaneously annihilate the embryonic disaster in a cryptic but not the less effective manner. This again is the superstition of ignorance.

But if the Chinaman were afflicted with this grotesque superstition, there would at least be some official explanation of it.

He might attribute the promised effect of salt spilling to his having offended the god of medicine by treating salt in a light hearted manner; the vanquishing of the evil forces by the above method he might attribute to the circumstance that he had put salt on the tail of the devil dodging behind his chair, thereby check-mating him. Cause and effect would be definite enough, and this again is the superstition of custom. But the manner in which the Chinese display this trait best is in their solicitude for ancestors.

Whole continents of thin air are peopled by spirits, which are by no means horrid attenuated things like our spirits, but

THE JUNK VOYAGE

substantial enough to have earthly desires; similarly there are vast companies of evil spirits just to level things up — monopolies in the spirit world are not to be encouraged.

So they build towers out in the fields and crown them with earthenware pots, into which any evil spirits drifting carelessly through the neighbourhood tumble; and they place stone lions handy to gobble them up as fast as they are caught.

Frequently there are no lions, but it only annoys a Chinaman to suggest that in such a case the pot might get full.

"You don't understand!" he says testily. "You don't understand it at all. That little pot will hold any number of spirits!"

And they employ geomancers to select suitable places for their graves which should be near water and shaded from the north or west, or perhaps from the south or east — it depends mainly on the geomancer.

And the graves themselves are objects of great care, especially new graves, for it is those spirits fresh to the shadow world which are particularly restless before settling down, as well as being more prone than the old hands to the tricks of devils.

Consequently one frequently sees little white flags stuck up leading from a novice's grave to the dead man's home, so that his spirit can find its way back when it desires to revisit the old haunts; and flags are sometimes stuck up leading in exactly the opposite direction also, the route being strewn with imitation sycee regardless of expense, in order to start devils off on a paper chase in the wrong direction, leaving the way clear for the good spirit: for everyone knows the magnetic attraction hard cash has for devils.

In this way the spirit may return unmolested to its home and slip back to its own quarters again without being waylaid, though it must have some near squeaks sometimes.

The 15th of each moon is set aside for attending the wants

of people in the other world, and at nightfall the family grave is visited and silver paper sycee or brown paper cash burnt.

For spirits are remittance men, and require their allowance every month in order to purchase the good things of the shadow world.

When the paper has disappeared in smoke and flame the transaction is regarded as complete, but what the commodities of the other world are, we are not told — iced drinks as like as not.

Of course, as I said before, they don't believe all this themselves, they only do it. As a rule, the regularity with which the native performs such peculiar ceremonies is an inverse measure of his knowledge concerning their use; but that of course is no hindrance why he should not go through the fashionable and traditional pantomime.

The scenery up the Tan was more interesting than any we had traversed hitherto, for the narrow river brawls noisily through a series of delightful limestone gorges, at this season covered with autumn flowers and tinted leaves.

A splendid stone embankment or causeway had been built half way through one gorge, though there seemed to be few people in the neighbourhood to use it.

But the numerous tsai-tsi crowning the mountain summits, telling of the days when the people had fled to the last strongholds at the rumoured approach of the dreaded T'ai-pings, and many ancient terraces on the mountain sides, now no longer cultivated, showed that this corner of Hupeh had once been far more densely populated. The trackers scrambled high up on the cliff face, where the opening of a cave home, also deserted, sometimes showed up, or along the boulders down below, and we found more to interest us on our daily walks. Nevertheless junk life at its best is wearisome, and we heaved a sigh of relief when we

THE JUNK VOYAGE

tied up off Kin-tsi-kuan, on the borders of Honan and Shensi, on 5th November. Three days were spent ashore, preparing for the serious work ahead, a stay made pleasant by the kindness of the missionaries, and on 9th November we started with four pack mules into the mountains.

2

OVER THE SIN-LING

FOLLOWING DEVIOUS back roads into the heart of the Sin-ling range we reached the obscure village of Luan-chuang, four stages from Kin-tsi-kuan, now finding ourselves on a trail hitherto untrodden by white men.

The scenery was delightful throughout, mountains stretching away in every direction, a billowy sea of rounded peaks and water-worn gullies, the village itself standing beside a noisy stream rattling through the main valley.

Many a sturdy hill was crowned by a ruined keep, the last resort of the villagers when the T'ai-ping rebels swept through southern Shensi, and perched on the summit of the highest mountain in the district was a temple, standing on tiptoe to heaven as it were. Patches of brown oak scrub or of green pine and fir woods covered many of the hillsides, and even late in November purple asters, golden chrysanthemums and other wild flowers made the hollows gay with colour.

We were received with open arms and open mouths, a wondering throng following us in close order through the street as children follow a circus, and to the accompaniment of much barking from the dogs and grunting from the pigs, we found an inn and settled down for ten days' hunting. On market days vast crowds attended our taxidermic demonstrations, standing six

OVER THE SIN-LING

deep round the open door, and though for the most part they were dumb with astonishment at what they saw, content just to stare with bulging eyes and gaping mouth, yet it was instructive to hear the awed remarks they occasionally ventured on since they permitted us a glimpse at our operations from their own point of view.

"Can you catch these?" we asked a small boy, pointing to a series of mice lying on the table.

"No, we don't eat them," was the naive reply.

The elders were more puzzled, and just a wee bit shocked but they rejected the theory of a mus diet.

"Fancy grown men, and foreign excellencies too, running after rats and mice! Why our little boys can catch them!" was what they said. But when a tariff had been drawn up, and they understood that money might be earned by bringing good specimens scruples were thrown to the wind and spades to the ground while husbandmen went dashing all over the country with incredible zeal to procure them.

Still, our business was a perpetual puzzle to them, for a museum was an idea they could not grasp. As soon as they realised that we were taking samples of their vermin to our own country they remarked with droll surprise: "Oh! then you have no rats and mice in your country," whereupon it was patiently pointed out to them that we had rats and mice, but that they were not the same as those, and the good folk scratched their heads over this unique communication for a long time. Moreover they were quite prepared to believe that the little creatures stuffed with cotton wool and penned out on a board to dry would come to life again when they (reached our mysterious country.

Autumn in the mountains of western China is glorious. Between the fierce heat of the summer, when all vegetation is parched and gasping, and winter with its dreadful monotony of limitless snow, withered grass, and naked trees, come three months of radiant days and crisp nights. Then the flowers bloom as though spring had come again; the faded vegetation, at dawn dripping with dew or sparkling with the first frost, turns many-coloured; persimmon trees laden with golden fruit deck the mountain slopes with spots of fire; and at night the moon, climbing up the sky, presently licks the tops of the black mountains and sends shafts of light down into the shadowy valley, where it glances on the white granite pebbles of the river bed and illuminates the rapids with streaks of dancing silver. Amongst the ever present crowd round our door many faces soon became familiar. In particular, two neatly dressed little school boys, sons of the village headman, were never tired of watching us, from the time school finished till closing time, and not infrequently they played truant all the morning, or slipped out of school while the master was not looking, in order to attend the meeting; for this little village of about five hundred inhabitants boasted two private and one temple school. It was in 1898 that the unfortunate Kwang Hsu issued the Imperial Edict which apparently sealed his doom decreeing that the old village temples should be transformed into schools and supported by the village, the scholar receiving a free education.

As we went along the street in the half light before dawn we frequently met boys trotting off to school and heard the medley of sounds made by twenty or thirty of them repeating their lessons aloud, all different and each in his own key; for in the village schools the boys still learn the Confucian classics by heart, and when , after several years of memorising, the time comes for some of it to be explained to the pupil, he has usually left school and gone to work in the fields, which perhaps accounts for the fact that so many villagers can neither read nor write.

In spite of Imperial indifference, however, it must not be

supposed that the people are themselves blind to the advantages of education. It is the golden dream of every Chinaman to become an official, and when that dream has faded in the father, it revives in the son; occasionally a whole family will starve in order to send a bright boy to school, that he may eventually climb the ladder of examinations that leads to office. But under the old regime no poor man could become an official though he were brilliant as da Vinci; it required a Croesus. Perhaps a day of better things has dawned recently.

In the mountains we met an old man of sixty-seven who had just returned from Hsian-fu with honour to his native village, and an M. A. degree to dangle after his name for the rest of his life; for he had been chosen out of forty-eight candidates — probably because the authorities knew he was too old ever to attain office.

Our cook was inclined to chaff the veteran, telling him that it would be years before a vacancy occurred, and that when it did he would have to go to Peking and disburse some five thousand taels as the price of his selection, for there are far more degree men awaiting office than there are vacancies to be auctioned. The cook feelingly added that he would be dead long before then, and certainly the old man didn't took to be worth five thousand taels to the sharks at Peking.

A row of tins emblazoned with coloured labels stood on our table and these caused the crowd infinite delight. "Have you beautiful things like that at home?" they asked, palpitating,

"Far more beautiful things," they were told, with a hint as to silver, glass and gold ornaments.

But there is a limit even to Chinese credulity; the beautiful shining tins with the coloured labels were there and could not be gainsaid but beyond that we were certainly taking advantage of their admiration to magnify things. No, they could now believe in gaudy tins, but no further.

ON THE ROAD TO TIBET

Then they asked us about the fire cart which they had heard went from Hankow to Peking in two days; and how far away it was to our country — though they found twenty thousand li beyond their comprehension of distance verging on the legendary; and they fingered our clothes and boots with intense curiosity, but most of all were they delighted with the traps and guns, the camp beds and a sponge. A cheap tin lantern also came in for much comment and not a little flattery having been mistaken at different times for a clock, the big foreign opium lamp and a thermometer. When it was lighted the natives fluttered around it with the importance of moths, and did not stint their admiration for a light which illuminated half the room.

As the news of our business was spread broadcast over the country and retailed forty or fifty li distant it gained in picturesqueness at the expense of accuracy, and some amusing results followed.

Bats for example were scarce and commanded a good price — thirty cash each. When therefore a man appeared with what purported to be a handkerchief full of them we were in ecstacies, and the reward was about to be handed over when something squeaked, a very big squeak for a bat. Suspicions were aroused, the handkerchief untied, and to our intense chagrin and surprise, out squirmed as well as they were able considering that their tails were tied together, an amorphous mass of domestic rats; which, flapping on the floor and attempting to depart in different directions, formed a sort of parallelogram of forces, the heavy handed resultant appearing from above in the guise of a foot. The poor man had walked thirty li to bring us a parcel of rats, though it is only fair to add that the mistake as to their being bats arose with our boy, and was not an intentional fraud.

The natives were not however invariably straightforward in their dealings, as we found on rejecting an excellent wild boar skin which was offered us, on the ground that without its skull, it was useless for scientific purposes. A few days later, in another village, a second man came forward with a wild boar skin and skull intact .as he informed us, in proof of which he unrolled the skin and showed us the skull lying loose inside.

It was a very large skin and a very small skull, and the most casual inspection suggested that the two were mutually exclusive, a suspicion confirmed by measurement. A more careful examination however, revealed the damaging fact that the skull was not that of a wild boar at all, but had belonged to a domestic hog, and further, that the skin was the identical one we had recently rejected!

It was an astute attempt at overreaching, but the wily native had paid too poor a compliment to the science of comparative anatomy.

However, our edict went forth not without effect, and specimens of the rarer animals were submitted to us daily, from Luan-chuang we proceeded a short distance up the valley to a lonely spot just under the watershed between the two great river systems of China, and here we settled down to work once more amongst the thick scrub of oak, hazel, birch, and chestnut which clothed the mountains, now rising to an altitude of about seven thousand feet.

The most interesting character here was our innkeeper's little daughter, a coy maiden of fourteen who was engaged to a young fellow we had met in Luan-chuang, though they had not yet seen each other; nor indeed is it customary for any engaged couple to do so in China till after the ceremony, which is chiefly of a gastronomic nature.

Previous to this the bridegroom will call for his bride and, heavily veiled, she will be carried in a chair, probably for the first time in her life, down the valley to his father's house, whereupon the feasting begins; and finally the groom will unveil his bride.

Poor fellow! This damsel is almost certain to develop a large goitre shortly, while her ignorance of everything beyond her own mountain acre is only paralleled by her ignorance of that acre itself; whereas the young man has been brought up in a market village and has been to school. We did hear a story of a young man whose father procured him an excellent wife during the famine which devastated Shensi in 1901, when wives could be bought cheaply. On unveiling her however, the bridegroom found to his consternation that the poor girl was terribly pockmarked, and incensed beyond words at the trick his father had played, he packed up his things and went straight off! He had lived long enough with foreigners to have an inkling that he was, after all, a free agent.

Yet this procedure is by no means so high handed as it appears at first sight; we regard marriage as a lottery; the Chinese eliminate the element of chance involved.

Experienced parents can make far better arrangements with an eye to future welfare than can callow youth, and by suspending the contract like a sword of Damocles continuously over the head of his expectant son, paterfamilias is in possession of a powerful weapon; when it falls, it is far less likely to cut him than some of his own choice.

A young man who has just begun to dip his hand into the bran pie of love and stir things around, fingers a variety of prizes always with the idea that the next will be nicer; and in the ensuing confusion he lets the best, which was probably the first, slip back into the bran.

It may be objected that such external interference is suicidal to the glamour of romance; but other things have long since taught us that all romances, except one's own, are very tawdry incidents.

OVER THE SIN-LING

Continuing our journey northwards, we crossed the main watershed at an altitude of only 4,600 feet and descended rapidly into the broad alluvial valley cf the Lo-ho, with its rich fields and prosperous villages — a strong contrast to the poverty on the other side. Soon we reached the coal district near Ching-ts'un, and here we found the people for the first time rude and noisy, displaying a sort of subdued hostility which chiefly gave vent to itself in the form of hustling curiosity and cries of "foreign devil," in a stage whisper.

However we only remained the night at Ching-t'sun, and next day continued across the valley and so into the mountains again. Thus the Sin-ling range is here seen to consist of two diverging ridges separating at a point some distance to the west, at the source of the Lo-ho.

Eastwards, where the Lo-ho joins the Yellow River in Honan, the range breaks up still more and descends gradually into the eastern plain, but the general trend remains the same.

These two ridges, separated by the Lo-ho, may be called the southern or Mang-ling. and the northern or Ching-ming, and it is the former and lower ridge which marks the boundary between the Yangtse and Yellow River basins.

On descending into the Lo valley we had found the character of the country changing, for the igneous rocks of which the southern ridge is composed here give place to limestone similar to that flanking the same ridge in the valley of the Tan River and still further north to low hills of sandstone and shale.

But having crossed the Lo-ho, a rapid and shallow stream, quite unnavigable, we immediately began the abrupt ascent of the Ching-ming, passing once more through limestone country, here developed into craggy pinnacles and cliffs slashed with deep gorges of great beauty and diversity, before again giving place to the igneous rocks composing the summit and northern slope of the ridge.

The Ching-ming, though of less extent, is, as already stated, of greater altitude than the main ridge, a rather paradoxical feature which may doubtless be attributed to greater precipitation on the more southern slope, since there is good reason to believe that northern Shensi had a far drier climate in times geologically recent; and in this connection it is worth noting that while all the peaks of the Mang-ling show the gracefully curved outline of water erosion, such is not the case with the similarly constituted Ching-ming, the pinnacled nature of which points at least in part to a dry denuding agent.

Just beneath the summit of the Ching-ming ridge we stopped again for a few days, the most noticeable feature of the country being the extraordinary virulence with which the trees in this district had been attacked by mistletoe, constituting quite a feature in the scenery. These trees in fact frequently looked as though in some peculiar foliage, so numerous were the bunches of the parasite hanging from them.

Setting out for the capital on 7th December, we reached the col at the summit of the Ching-ming ridge which rises so precipitously above the great plain of the Wei river, the same day, and from an altitude of nearly 8,000 feet we looked southwards over the cloud swamped valley of the Lo-ho to the Mang-ling mountains already powdered with snow, or northwards over the great loess plain to the silver bow of the Yellow River itself and the Shansi mountains in a blur of haze beyond.

Continuing over the ridge we descended six thousand feet in a few hours, and at length emerged from the Sin-ling mountains on to the plain, pursuing our way to Hwa-yin-miao on the great west road which we reached in the evening after a long day.

This little city, four stages east of the provincial capital, is chiefly noted for the old Taoist temple which gives its name to the place, one of the finest of its kind in the country; and from this temple we looked over the quiet tree clad courts to see the sun set in a gloomy blaze behind the strange and awesome crags of Wha-san, one of the five sacred mountains of China.

Since setting out from Kin-tsi-kuan we had now been twenty-nine days in the mountains, of which nine had been spent on the road; and while it is impossible to estimate distances accurately, owing to the mountainous nature of the route, which is continuously ascending and descending thousands of feet, we had already covered about two hundred miles.

3

The Great Plain

On the morrow we ascended Wha-san, the flowery mountain. Viewed from Hwa-yin-miao this truncated column of rock seems to project almost vertically above the irregular ridge of the Ching-ming, two immense precipices flanking its tilted razor edge, which is crater shaped and culminates at either end in a pinnacle, that to the west being the higher. The ascent is made up a steep slit-like gully which evidently owes its formation to the peculiar jointing of this granite, causing it to exfoliate vertically in huge slabs. At the head of the gully we found ourselves at the base of the great west cliff which towers unbroken to the ridge, three thousand feet above, and by zigzagging gradually upwards and backwards towards the summit of the lower, or eastern precipice, we surmounted it by means of a long and steep chimney running diagonally across the rock face. From the bottom of this narrow chimney, to the summit of the east precipice, and along the whole length of the precipitous ridge to the western apex of the mountain, steps have been laboriously cut out of the solid rock and iron stanchions, supporting chains, driven in, for the convenience of pilgrims, — a vast and hazardous undertaking which must have been done by some virile race in times long past. Rock ladders, when vertical, are not the easiest things in the world to ascend, even when accompanied by chains, yet it is

THE GREAT PLAIN

not, indeed, the difficulty of the ascent that is memorable, but the ingenuity with which the seemingly insurmountable difficulties have been overcome. Any active person gifted with moderately steady nerves can now ascend Wha-san, but it would puzzle most of us to climb it without the aid of the steps and chains!

At an altitude of nearly 8,000 feet, not far from the summit, we spent the night in a temple enclosed by a forest of grand old pines, twisted and bent with years, our intention being to continue our way to the famous iron roofed temple at the summit on the morrow.

But fate willed otherwise, for it snowed heavily during the night, and next morning the whole mountain was wreathed in such a pall of mist that our only course was to descend at once to the plain, which descent down the knife edge and rock ladders, slippery with ice and flanked by precipices on either hand, was not without its thrills. However, we reached Hwa-yin-miao in safety.

At the time of the hwoi in the third moon, that is, in April, as many as two thousand pilgrims may be sleeping up on the mountain, every temple being occupied; but at this season there were not more than a score of priests in residence, and many of the temples were closed.

On the following day we set out across the plain for Hsian-fu. The great plain of the Wei river is part of the vast loess district of western and central China, which, stretching through the provinces of Kansu, Shensi and Shansi to the confines of Honan and Chili, covers an area of not less than twenty thousand square miles, exclusive of outliers further east. North of the yellow river in Shansi, the deposit attains a maximum thickness of at least a thousand feet, but in Shensi it is of less depth.

Seen from the hillside the loess plain descends in sweeping terraces apparently in uninterrupted succession to the Wei river.

This is an illusion, however, for in reality the seemingly level surface is broken up by sunken streams, roads and yawning holes or gorges which have been worn down frequently to a depth of two hundred feet.

These features are due to the vertical cleavage of the deposit, in conjunction with the fact that the loess is not quite continuous throughout, being interstratified at different horizons with rubble beds which check the downward weathering in one place while it continues in another. Thus the country has acquired this curious platform structure on a large scale, while wherever running water appears, its detailed structure presents the still more extraordinary feature of sudden almond shaped ravines, thinning out as abruptly as they began, or of knife cut gullies, like immense swallow-holes.

The fertility of this seemingly starved drift soil is remarkable.

With the first spring showers the dun coloured plain leaps suddenly into life, vigorous green life, pushing up and thrusting itself out every where from below; moreover the soil is cropped two and even three times a year without any systematic rotation.

On the cliff faces, a white efflorescence of salt may frequently be observed, but it must not be concluded that the surface loam itself is saline, for the porous nature of the soil determines the deep seated origin of its salts. The first rain however establishes capillary connection with the subterranean moisture, thus tapping the almost inexhaustible resources of the soil, the necessary salt supply diffusing to the surface, where it frequently crystalizes out.

On the other hand, should there be a dearth of rain during one or two years, the crops fail for lack of this connection being established, and Shensi has in consequence been periodically visited by the most awful famines. Every three years, the people say, is a small famine, the spring crops failing; every ten years,

THE GREAT PLAIN

a large famine, both spring and autumn crops failing. And the actual cycle corresponds pretty closely with this. But road making in such a country is another matter, and anyone who has seen the great west road in either wet or dry weather will not easily forget it; like most of the Imperial highways, it seems to belong to the age of the Great Wall and the Grand Canal, and needs mending.

During the rains it is a ghastly swamp through which the panting, shivering mules crawl up to their gurths, thrashed mercilessly through the mudholes which threaten to swallow them up completely, by the yelling drivers; during the dry weather when the caked mud has got thoroughly mixed up, the entire road blanketed in a seething cloud of impalpable powder, through which the choking mules still pant and writhe. So the great road winds its way across the Empire, a monument of inefficiency.

In this part of the country cave dwellings are to be met with everywhere, sometimes scores together. Traversing the plain, it is not uncommon to come with such startling suddenness upon a village lying far below one's feet, that the astonished Gulliver unconsciously stumbles back a pace from the edge of the breach. There at the bottom of a deep canyon, the sides of which are honeycombed through and through with caves, lies a human rabbit warren.

It is impossible to travel in the interior of China without unpleasant experiences sooner or later, and every traveller has stories to tell of chairs being upset, junks foundering, and similar untoward accidents. We were now to taste of the bitter cup ourselves, for the first but by no means for the last time.

The start estwards was not propitious, for it snowed in a sloppy manner throughout the day, and leaving the mules to bring the kit along as fast as they could, we pushed ahead. By the time we had done twenty miles we felt ready to stop, and turned into a wayside inn to await food and blankets.

Two hours freezing however sufficed to convince us that the mules had taken a side road and were not coming our way at all, whereupon we turned out into the night and started in pursuit, in order to catch them at the next stopping place, twenty miles further on.

Happily the horrid monotony of the loess plain was now screened behind snow and darkness, and we picked our way rapidly through the mud. Sometimes our footsteps echoed noisily under a gateway and we went sliding and stamping over the cobbles of a sleeping village; sometimes the wreck of a temple lurched dismally out of the whiteness to be as quickly immersed. And there it was oblivion and the deeply rutted road gleaming irregularly through it again. It was dismal work, but we marched into Tschi-chin at 1 a.m. in pretty good form, and having aroused every inn-keeper in the place, only to learn that our mules had not arrived, we gained admittance to an inn by dint of much exercise on the door, and for the rest of the night huddled shivering round a small pan of charcoal.

The mules turned up at ten o'clock next morning, looking rather the worse for wear too, for they had lost the way in the darkness; but in half an hour we were ready for the road again, reaching Wei-nan that day.

On 12th December, we reached Lin-t'ung, famous for its hot sulphur springs. The late Empress Dowager stayed at the baths here during her flight from Peking, and we had the honour of occupying the same room which she had graced. I often, as a child, when visiting Windsor Castle (unofficially of course) gazed upon beds in which whole squadrons of kings and queens had slept, and wondered whether those uneasy crowned heads used to rest on the dainty filigree pillows as conscience free as

THE GREAT PLAIN

mine would; but in my wildest dreams I had never expected to occupy the same bath as an Empress of China.

Next day we were early on foot for Hsian, and after crossing a small river by a bridge built entirely of milestones, and topping a rise, we presently saw through a haze of dust scattered up by the strings of jostling carts, the great towers of the east gate.

To north, south, and east stretches the vast plain, thrown into puckers by the grave mounds which thrust themselves up like sugar loaves everywhere, and relieved only by scattered villages with half demolished walls; across it winds the great road, smoking with the dust of the west bound traffic.

Suddenly there seems to rise out of the ground before us a huge wall, bristling with rows of watch towers, and we find ourselves outside a large village, nestling under the shadow of the wall; this is the east suburb.

To north and south the plain stretches on in limitless monotony. Approach the city from any direction, the plain ends abruptly under that immense rampart, except where the four compact mudwalled suburbs protrude from it like warts.

Probably no thriving city in the world has a history so full of stirring incident as has the capital of Shensi.

Emerging from the legendary period of Chinese history famous as the birthplace of Fu-hsi, who three thousand years ago taught the people the use of salt, whereby they lost the gills and hair with which they had hitherto been adorned, how to fish and cook, and to keep flocks, we find it, under the name of Cha'ng-an, the capital of the Empire from B.C. 206 till A.D. 605, when the capital was removed to Honan; and as such it figures largely in the early dynastic wars, revolutions and invasions which from time to time decimated the Middle Kingdom.

Hsian has also with some show of reason been identified with the place where Aladdin found the treasure cave. Some distance from the city are a number of immense tumuli, the graves of early emperors, and it was into one of these that Aladdin is supposed to have been taken by the geniis.

As was customary in those times, treasure was buried with the departed emperor, and perhaps his chief ministers also, those that were unable to accommodate their span of life to his naturally, being helped to do so artificially with Procrustean simplicity; just as the death of an Inca of Peru implied the self-immolation of hundreds in his household.

In recent history Hsian is chiefly notable as the refuge of the late Empress-Dowager, after her flight from Peking in 1900. The most interesting sight in the city is the Pei-lin, where stands the famous Nestorian tablet, recording the establishment in China of the illustrious religion of Syria, during the T'ang dynasty, A.D. 781.

This monument, safe at last let us hope, has had a chequered career since its discovery during some excavations beyond the west gate.

After being disentombed, it was set up outside the city, but so little notice did it attract, that before attention was again directed towards it, the turtle which serves as a pedestal for the tablet was already buried in the drifting loess, and it seemed in a fair way to sink back into that oblivion from which it had been temporarily rescued.

Thereupon representations were made by foreigners to the central government that such a unique record might be properly cared for, and the government complied by allotting the sum of one thousand taels for the erection of a suitable pavilion to receive it.

But money allotted in Peking and destined for a place as far distant as Hsian must trickle through the sievelike pockets of a large number of officials en route, and by the time the treasury was

THE GREAT PLAIN

a thousand taels poorer, Hsian was only a hundred taels richer; and by the time that hundred taels had been accommodated so as to please everybody, the contractors were only ten taels better off than before; whereupon they erected an open bamboo canopy which was demolished by the first wind.

We next hear of the tablet as the cynosure of a journalist, doubtless a man of innocent designs though of covetous instincts.

Fascinated to a pitch of fanaticism, he proceeded to have an exact copy of the memorial made on the spot, and it was presumably this cumbersome reproduction that he transported as far as Hankow, where, it is said, it yet lies in a godown.

But by this time the authorities had become thoroughly alarmed, and getting wind of the affair they removed the monument into the city, placing it in the Pei-lin, where it stands with the Confucian Classics, engraved on thirteen tablets, a portrait of the sage himself, similarly engraved, and many other famous memorial stones of great antiquity.

The Chinese had at last realised the principle in human nature which determines that a thing becomes of value as soon as somebody else wants it.

Worthy of note also is the Mohammedan mosque, dating from the second century; for Hsian is the great centre of the Mohammedans in China.

Standing in the midst of the country overrun during the great Mohamedan rebellion of 1861-1876, Hsian held out while every other city and village for leagues around was eased to the ground.

These pleasant days of sightseeing in the capital were spent with Mr. and Mrs. Shorrock of the Baptist Mission, who entertained us with the utmost hospitality.

After seeing the missions at work in the interior, one cannot but feel that the prejudice felt in many circles towards missionaries has its foundation almost entirely in misconception, and is largely based on a popular fallacy.

But while extraordinary misapprehensions are prevalent on the coast concerning mission work, it must be conceded that the intolerant attitude towards people holding different views, adopted by many missionaries in the treaty ports, militates against any sympathy and widens the breach. The universal argument is, I believe, that missionaries are busybodies. who come out to China to try and root out the national religion, forcing instead an alien one down the throat of the reluctant Chinaman, who has after all done very well with his own for centuries; furthermore, that the result of this coercion is a spirit of unrest culminating in a hatred of the foreigner and his ways, and finally active riot.

But what is the national religion of China? Buddhism was introduced from India during the first century, and has been so mutilated since that there are really no Buddhists left in China. Those who periodically visit the Buddhist temples and toss their cash to the sharks waiting to snap them up, go there to ask for rain or riches, sunshine or health, and are no more Buddhists than are those persons who pay perfunctory visits to church, Christians.

That it is of extraneous origin is of little consequence; most religions are. There is scarcely a religion of standing to-day that has not migrated from its place of origin to centres, renounced by its former zealots.

But that the new religion should at once have come into contact with two others already established, suggests that it was destined to fall rapidly into that decline which has overtaken so many things in China which are found to be ornamental but not useful. The religion now foisted upon the world as Buddhism is a wolf in sheep's clothing — and a very sick wolf too.

THE GREAT PLAIN

Religion is as fully subject to the laws of evolution as is life itself, being in fact a part of life, and it would be strange indeed if, under the changed conditions, this one had retained its individuality. As it is, Buddha himself would not recognise the state religion of China. Nor can one call such a neglected creed in any sense national, since from the time of its introduction it has been only passively submitted to by the laity (who being at heart either pantheists or atheists — there is little difference — are capable of absorbing a pot-pourri of religions), its metamorphosis being entirely due to a process of natural decay, and not to any startling reformations or adaptations from within; while the priests regard a shorn head and gray ma-kua chiefly as a sanctuary from the penalty of crime.

Again, has China done so very well by herself for centuries? One can hardly think so when a usurper sits on her throne, and no sooner was she brought face to face with something new, in the shape of western progress, than she found herself in difficulties.

Being insufficiently plastic to adapt herself to new conditions, she could yet hardly hope to continue to infinity as she was, and though everyone must agree that China can and must greatly strengthen herself, by climbing out of the old groove, the period of transition is an unpleasant one.

Taoism could never have been a religion in the sense of being the inevitable solace which we believe humanity unconsciously seeks, and the corrupt Taoism of to-day is merely a grotesque philosophy; while Confucianism never pretended to take the place of a religion at all, though it is the purest ethical code which has survived as a national product.

On the other hand, Buddhism has simply wallowed in Taoism, Taoism in Confucianism, and the last named, the pedestal upon which the creed of every Chinaman stands, reeks of both.

Of their reverence for ancestors we have already had

examples.

It is this irreconcilable element, the infertile hybrid of a materialism which deifies ancestors with a superstition which identifies hopelessly imbecile deities with every manifestation of nature, that the traveller finds so incongruous. For what is the use of exalting one's ancestors to the rank of gods, and degrading one's gods to the rank of mortals? In trying to be everything the Chinaman is nothing. He professes Buddhism, bows down to Confucius, and practices polytheism; he stocks an invisible, but apparently material world, with the immortal spirits of his venerated ancestors, and regulates many actions of his life in accordance with their welfare.

He has achieved the ultimate solace by the back-door, without the trouble of striving after any ideal; like picking plums out of a snap-dragon with a pair of gloves on. New lamps for old, and when the old have lapsed into the empty condition of those in charge of the delinquent virgins, it is a pretty good bargain.

When a man can neither read nor write, he may be steeped in ecclesiasticism without possessing one jot of religious sense, and this applies to most of the mountain population of China, to millions in fact.

Hence, can they once wrench themselves free of their morbid conservatism, they lap up a real doctrine with avidity. And there lies the first trouble, for it is just these people who are beyond even the fringe of mission influence. There is no precedent in all history for believing that a nation will rise in riot and murder people simply because a new religion is being offered them. Even Nero did not slay the Christians because he objected to their religious views, for in religious matters Nero was a most tolerant man.

There was always something behind it, and so there is in China.

THE GREAT PLAIN

Men have fought, and tortured, and murdered their fellow men in order to make them accept a religion, but have never yet done so in order to get rid of one.

The Mohammedans, who are racially distinct from the Chinese, are the only people in China who can be said to have a self-contained religion, and they are the rarest of proselytes.

Lastly, it is rather ridiculous to assert, as people do, that Christianity is rolled up into a ball so to speak, like a brickbat concealed in a stocking, and the native smitten on the head with it till it penetrates.

The very term of derision with which the average native greets the new convert, namely that he is eating the foreigners' doctrine, suggests nothing but peace and repose.

Above all however will the missionaries of the twentieth century be remembered for the incalculable impetus they have given to education in China, and for the humanitarianism they display in tending and caring for the sick. There is no starving the body and feeding the soul on indigestible facts, which would naturally tend to give a hungry man the stomach ache, that is if an empty stomach can ache; it is the propagation of the gospel as it was carried abroad by the twelve apostles — healing the sick, clothing the naked, and comforting the lonely.

Occasionally it is true one does meet a person who appears to have been quite recently dispensing butter — probably adulterated, and local gossip, likewise adulterated, at the village grocery store which is also the post office; who having been saved with such an abrupt jerk that it seems to have wrenched something loose inside, has come rushing out to China, hot to murder everybody else by dispensing the word of God, still adulterated.

He regards alcohol as so much prussic acid and the use of it as premeditated suicide; he speaks proudly of his conversion (ominous word) which implied exchanging an obsequious air behind the counter for a pompous air in front of the heathen, and looks with arctic contempt on any other profession than his own.

The gentlemen of this school are fanatical, the ladies — for it is a co-educational establishment, prim. They have one virtue — sincerity, a virtue which the most rabid will admit covers many defects; better a sincere crank than a hypocrite; and perhaps the worst that can be said of them is that they mean well, for with an immense output of energy, they further the cause very little; as in the case of the steam engine, some ten per cent, of the power is expended in driving the engine, the other ninety per cent, being dissipated in hot air. But these people are quite the exception.

We also paid a visit to the Roman Catholic mission, and were shown over the premises by one of the Franciscan fathers, though so hospitable was he that I began to fear there was as much difficulty in store for this good man as the camel experienced in trying to assume a filiform disguise; for here were great possessions, nor was even mild asceticism conspicuously cultivated.

The atmosphere of that mission, the white capped sisters of mercy, the gorgeous pomp of the cathedral, above all the clear old Mere Superieure, carried me back through seventeen years to a summer spent in the south of France, during a brief part of which time I was sent to a convent school to learn French.

I had a gay time, and they stood it for a week while I periodically burst into the girls' schoolroom bringing caterpillars and other frivolous pets which I had found in the garden, to the Mere Superieure, who didn't want them.

But the climax was reached when I danced into the chapel during mass, to fetch a little girl of whom I was very fond, to play hide-and-seek with me in the grounds.

The Roman Catholics are a susceptible people, and my crime

could not be condoned. I was expelled forthwith, the Mere Superieure herself taking me back to my mother carriage paid. "Il a le diable dans ses jambes," she said, with tears in her eyes, thinking of my enormities, and my mother was very much ashamed of me for quite a week. No jam for tea, and everything I wanted must be asked for in French! There were quite a number of things I had to go without — it was very distressing.

But I didn't cry, though I liked the convent school and the little French girl; in fact expulsion from my first school was always a source of hilarity to me.

Poor Mere Superieure! I taught her more English ways than she ever taught me French words.

A few days later our stay at Hsian drew to a close, and bidding good-bye to our kind friends at the mission, we turned our faces westwards once more.

4

Tai-Pei-San

It was 22nd December when we took to the loess road again, our object being to recross the Sui-ling range in the neighbourhood of Tai-pei-san, and reach Han-chong-fu on the headwaters of the Han river.

Three days later, near Chow-tse, we came across the first opium fields we had seen, but it is doubtful whether those little seedlings were destined to flower; probably they would all be ploughed up within a few months.

It is an old, old story, but the present vigorous campaign against opium dates back only three years, to a memorial signed by over a thousand missionaries in China, which was presented to the Imperial Throne; and then came the opium conference in Shanghai.

Previous to this protracted negotiations with Great Britain had led to an arrangement whereby it was agreed that the importation of Indian opium should cease pari passu with the extinction of the indigenous plant, so that if in ten years China herself was free, India also would cease to import opium; and in 1906 was issued the famous edict which was to sweep corruption from the land.

The Imperial government proceeded promptly and with discretion in the matter. Three widely separated provinces were selected, and the cultivation of the poppy with their boundaries prohibited, provincial governments being at the same time enjoined to deal stringently with offenders, who certainly had no cause for being ignorant of the edict, copies of which were posted, according to custom, on every village temple.

In the following year three more opium growing provinces came under the ban, and now the velvet glove has been drawn off, and the cultivation of the poppy has been everywhere forbidden in no uncertain terms.

The popular idea has arisen, however, that because China herself grows opium, therefore she is in favour of, or at least indifferent to, the continuation of the habit.

But opium has only been cultivated in China within the memory of living men, and there can be no question that the upper class of the nation have always been vigorously opposed to the vice, a fact strikingly borne out by the vigilance with which the officials make their tours of inspection through the provinces, now that a scheme likely to lead to fruitful results has been promulgated. And woe to the farmer discovered growing opium on the sly!

On the other hand is China to be entirely exculpated? Her coffers enriched by colossal imports, her people demanding the article set tantalisingly before them, can she, when the day of retribution for tins absorbing vice inevitably comes, with justice turn on those who have pandered to her weakness and say: "You taught us this! Our blood be upon your head"!

Can the man who takes a serpent to his bosom blame the serpent for striking him? Is ignorance accepted as an excuse for crime?

Arraigned before a British court, the most just tribunal in the world, what verdict would be passed on China for this holocaust of misery? Nothing less than accessory after the fact, itself a serious indictment.

It is unpleasant to inveigh against one's native land, but the evidence goes to show that part of the stigma of having taught China the opium habit, lies at the door of the old country; not indeed for having refused to exercise an arbitrary control over the tillers of her soil in the Indian Empire, or over her merchants who were then seeking with undaunted courage to open new markets to the world, and build up our mercantile marine – no country which stands for a free people could possibly entertain such a project; but for permitting the smuggling of opium into Canton to proceed unchecked and distend year by year, a business which perhaps did more to propagate the traffic in opium than any other combination of circumstances.

It was a blunder at a critical time, but was due more to our inability to cope with a movement on such a magnificent scale, than to any indifference to the consequences of such a corrupt practice.

At the close of what was called the second "opium war" in 1860, China, realising that she was not sufficiently strong to prevent the importation of the Indian drug, decided to grow her own supply in the hope of throttling the overseas trade; and this step she took in self-defence, fully resolved that, having quenched its importation she would be able to turn her attention to the home product, and exterminate that also.

But charity begins at home, and China failed to recognise a new factor in Political Economy, namely that, in the case of necessities, supply is not more than equal to demand, but that with luxuries on the other hand, demand is equal to supply. Tea merchants spring into existence every month without hustling things, but no one is rash enough to put a new soap on the market; tobacco is sold in a hundred forms but there are no blends of salt. We can get along very well without the necessities of life, but it would kill most of us to go without its luxuries.

So China's single-handed effort failed, and the last state was worse than the first. But many things tend to show that the day of opium is on the wane, not least amongst which is the fact that the price of the drug has advanced during the past year, from two hundred cash an ounce to its weight in silver, so that many who were formerly opium smokers can now only afford to chew or drink it, possibly a more disgusting, certainly a less absorbing, vice.

In Kansu, however, around Min-chow and again further South near Kai-chow, there was a fairly extensive cultivation of the forbidden plant, though there is no reason to argue a hopeless situation from this.

Kansu is the most isolated of all the provinces, an immense area without railways, and almost without water communication or telegraphs.

In such a country reforms naturally travel more slowly than decrees, and the latter travel slowly enough, since we were assured in Min-chow that the three-year-old edict prohibiting opium cultivation had only been promulgated there this year!

As is not generally known, the proclamation caused an incipient riot in Lan-chow, the provincial capital, in 1909, and the equivocal attitude of the Viceroy, who attempted to appease the wrath of the people by a clumsy compromise which virtually amounted to surrender, was speedily followed by his degradation. It is to be hoped that the new Viceroy of Shen-kan will deal more effectively with the situation.

That a Viceroy in western China is in a sufficiently autocratic position to enforce his orders, should he so wish, is strickingly borne out in the results obtained by H.E. Chao, Viceroy of Szechwan, who has so completely exterminated a plant which till recently covered thousands of acres, that during more than three months spent in this province, during which time we travelled hundreds of miles, we did not see a single opium poppy. Chao Er-hsung is the type of man China is in need of just now. Moderate in his designs, enlightened in his policy, and ruthless in his will, he stamped out what threatened to be a serious opium riot in south eastern Szechwan last year, almost before it had begun, and had the ring-leaders executed without mercy.

As the new movement is gradually absorbed from the coast and penetrates towards the west, it must inevitably be absorbed by Kansu, isolated as it is, and we may shortly expect this province also to profit by the example of the pioneers, and reap the benefit.

On Christmas day we left Chow-tsi and struck due south to the mountains, spending Christmas night at the foot of the pass.

There was only one room in the inn, and we sat down to our Christmas dinner, of which the "piece de resistance" was an immature plum pudding, in an atmosphere as dense as a London fog; the native guests, servants and inn people who crowded round seemed even more interested in the way our eyes streamed with water from the smoke of the wood fire, than they were at the melancholy hilarity of Christmas fare in the mountains.

Our attempt to get over the mountains next day proved abortive, for the mules were unable to follow the trail, and after six hours' march over difficult paths slippery with ice, we were forced to return to our starting point, which we reached shortly before midnight.

Next day we started west once more, and three days later found another pass which seemed practicable; and on the last day of the month we reached Ling-t'ai-miao, in the neighbourhood of Tai-pei-san. During the intense cold of early January we made our first ascent of Tai-pei, in the company of several native

TAI-PEI-SAN

hunters, and settled down in a small open cave at an altitude of ten thousand feet.

Here, rolled in our sheepskins and blankets, we passed the first bitter night, while it snowed furiously throughout, blowing into the cave and covering us with a fine powder; and next day an impenetrable veil of snow mist confined us to the cave.

The cold was very severe. A bottle of ink froze solid, so that it was impossible to write: even when it was thawed out, the ink froze on the pen in a moment; a cup of hot tea put down on the ground was covered with a film of ice in a few minutes, and if we put our feet to the fire our backs froze, while as soon as we turned our backs to it our feet froze. There was only one warm place, and that was on the fire itself.

That night however the stars blazed in the crystal sky and on the morrow the sun illuminated the ocean of cloud away down in the valley 8,000 feet below us. In a few hours we had attained an altitude of twelve thousand feet, and before continuing further, a weird religious ceremony was now enacted by the guide, in order to ensure success.

Laying the four native guns on a board, and lighting some incense which was thereupon stuck in the snow, the old man began to talk so fast and vehemently that I felt sure he must have an accident with his mouth before long; but no, he had it all off just as easily as you or I could say the multiplication table, with never a hitch.

Meanwhile he was tossing into the air two pieces of wood shaped like the two valves of mussel shell, watching how they had to fall in a particular manner of course, but nothing daunted that old man. If they fell the wrong way, he picked them up and tossed them into the air again, and it is certain he threw them up so many times that by the law of chance they must have fallen in every conceivable attitude several times over.

Whenever they fell the wrong way the other hunters yelled with laughter, and made needlessly facetious remarks to the poor old man, who was certainly doing his best for them; it was most indecorous behaviour.

The final spasm was the quaintest of all, however, for the supplicant, becoming suddenly as spry as a little school miss, did a capital step dance over the guns as they lay on the snow, tip-toeing slyly among them and waving his legs aloft in a burst of simple joy; and at last, taking each gun and passing it over one leg and under the other, as though indulging in calisthenics, handed it back to its owner, at the same time looking carefully at the sky and telling us that it would be all right.

We were glad to hear it. We had stood nearly knee-deep in the snow for a half an hour, watching this appeal to the gods, and it was satisfactory to know that a wireless had been received from them with so little delay.

After this we scrambled across serews, slid down snow slopes, and picked our way through deep drifts out on to the wildest ridges for many hours till late in the afternoon we reached a particularly desolate knife edge, all boulders and fir trees, dipping suddenly down into deep gullies on either hand.

Crouching behind a rock, at the beginning of this spur, the old hunter made a sign to us, and looking cautiously over the ledge we saw, not fifty yards away amongst the rocks and trees, a dozen or more huge long haired animals, unsuspicious, calmly feeding, the oxen we had come so far to hunt.

First one showed up, then another as they came closer and closer, ignorant of the fact that they were watched, while we trembled with excitement.

The hunter whispered his plans to surround the herd as rapidly as possible, but before anything was done, the American, who had our only rifle, opened fire, even then with a magazine rifle, it seemed child's play to hit them at forty yards range, but he gave such a brilliant exhibition of how to put bullets between a row of barn doors as it were — a fancy turn which would look pretty in the hippodrome but which hardly comes within the province of big game hunting — that we got nothing for our trouble.

At the first shot, a wild stampede from the ridge into the gully followed, and the sight of these unwieldy beasts bounding down the precipice and leaping from rock to rock with the greatest agility, was a memorable one. Late as it was, we followed the trail down the gully for some time, but being jammed full of large boulders, slippery with ice and covered with a treacherous layer of snow, we were soon compelled to relinquish the chase. Eventually we reached the cave after nightfall, and sat round a roaring fire drying our clothes.

What fine fellows these hunters were! All night long they sat round the fire passing their two-foot pipes from mouth to mouth, telling stories, and occasionally curling up for a short sleep; all day long they tracked their quarry with unerring skill, camping on the ground where they stopped, if necessary, and continuing with daylight. Their home-made match-lock guns were the most remarkable pieces of ordnance — six feet of gas piping tied to a bamboo. It took about five minutes to load one, and two or three more to fire it, and you could almost dodge the slugs as you saw them coming. Yet they did extensive execution at thirty paces, especially to the gunner, who, since the guns had no stock, got his cheek cut open at every discharge.

The following day was spent in tracking the herd, and though our efforts proved unavailing, two of the hunters tracked and shot a vagrant animal not far from the cave, and we skinned it next morning as it lay.

It was a medium sized male, weighing about four hundred

catties — say five hundred pounds, and it took four of us nearly five hours' work to rip the skin off; but the meat turned out to be first class beef.

On the fifth day we returned to the valley with the spoil, and a few days later came the news that the hunters had shot two more oxen on the far slopes of Tai-pei.

Accordingly we started up once more with the intention of spending the night on the mountain, skinning the two animals on the following day, and returning to the valley by moonlight.

We were better equipped on the expedition too, for ordinary nailed boots being utterly useless on the ice slopes previously encountered, we had taken a hint from the hunters, wrapping our feet in coarse woollen cloth to turn the snow, and wearing straw sandals to which were strapped iron spikes.

Eight hours' climbing brought us to the highest point we had yet attained, some 13,000 feet, and through the fast gathering darkness we looked across to the white summit of Tai-pei, gleaming wanly now and then between clouds of rolling mist.

At this time it was snowing, and I was alone with one of the coolies, some few hundred yards behind the party; next minute they were swallowed up amongst the trees and darkness.

Leaving the peak we had reached, the trail now led along a forested ridge, and after traversing a long snow slope, brought us to a gully, terminating in a shallow saddle, a few hundred feet below the summit of Tai-pei itself; and up this gully a stinging blast of icy wind was roaring, whipping up the snow, obliterating the trail, and singing through our clothes as though they had been muslin. Scudding clouds hid the moon, and time after time I was off the trail, plunging knee deep into the snow drifts. So for an hour we struggled along up the gully, though the cold of that arctic hurricane was almost unbearable; it seemed to freeze one's very senses and lacerated one's face painfully.

However we reached the saddle at last, and found ourselves on the rock serees, treacherously slippery with ice, but to some extent sheltered from the murderous wind; we were still following the trail, though numbed as I was, progress was painfully slow and dangerous falls frequent.

Another half hour and the end came; the trails diverged, my coolie, who was leading, took the wrong one, and at eight o'clock, after ten hours' climbing, we stopped exhausted, unable or unwilling to go further.

Choosing a spot under some stunted larches, as much out of the wind as possible, we at last, after many unsuccessful attempts with flint and steel on account of the gale, lit a fire and huddled round it; and there on the mountain side, at an altitude of nearly 12,000 feet, amidst wind and snow, without food or covering, we passed the night.

From time to time gusts of terrible wind swept down a gully close at hand, and roaring through the trees, chilled us to the bone; many a time I rose, stiff with cold, and broke branches from the trees to keep up the fire that alone made the night endurable.

At last, the full moon, having marched with leaden footsteps across the sky, set, and I dozed; not long afterwards the white peaks to the east began to show up in the grayness; the fire burned low; a bird whistled in the larches overhead, and I awoke. It was dawn.

With daylight I set out slowly for the village, and reaching it in eight hours, enjoyed a meal as only a ravenous person can.

Meanwhile the party had reached the shelter on the previous night, had skinned the animals next day, and got back to the inn at eleven o'clock the same night, having descended the mountain by the light of the full moon. Several characters in Ling-t'ai-miao impressed us not a little, foremost amongst these unique persons being a man named Chong, headman of the village; having earned his implacable hatred for some mysterious breach of etiquette, he proceeded to make matters unpleasant for us as far as lay in his power.

Not only did he put up the price of everything in his shop for our especial benefit — a sort of preferential tariff in fact, but by means of threats and bribes he attempted to make every other shopkeeper, and even itinerant pedlars, do the same; for hated and feared as Chong was in the village, he was king of the castle because he had the money. In Europe the man behind the money bags can do a good deal, but in China he can do anything.

Chong however was now dealing with foreigners, and he soon found himself before Dr. Smith, who threatened to have him taken to the yamen, unless he mended his ways; whereupon he cringed and attempted to regain our goodwill with clumsy artifices.

But retribution was at hand, and Chong awoke one night to find his k'ang on fire, and all his clothes burning.

Evidently he had offended the god of fire, so he now had to spend some money preparing theatricals to propitiate the wrathful deity. A platform would be erected near the little temple, and the god's eyes anointed with the blood of a rooster, to enable him to see round the corner — a peculiar optical property of chicken's blood, doubtless connected with triple refraction and Chang-shi would make night hideous till the god was satisfied. When we last heard of Chong, he was engaged in an undignified law suit with his mother-in-law.

Amongst the baby brigade who crowded round our barn door, a tiny toddler of three, who was never tired of leaning over the door-step and watching us at work, was a perpetual puzzle.

Though evidently belonging to the inn, yet she was always called the little stranger, and was disgracefully treated; and upon inquiry, the innkeeper satisfied our curiosity with the following

TAI-PEI-SAN

explanation of her name and presence. He had, he said, been blessed with a son and daughter, but his daughter had died, and his son had rebelled and run away.

Left with no provision for old age, he and his wife hit upon the device of buying the "little stranger" and bringing her up as their own child, so that when the couple were too old for work, any young fellow might have her on the understanding that he took her foster parents under his roof also.

Thus does the Chinaman seek a prop for his old age! One day we caught the old woman, who was a hag of the vilest type, actually beating the little girl over the head and face with a stick!

Poor little grub in rags! Her lot could not have been a merry one; yet she was always smiling, and on being taken notice of as she watched us at work, would crow as happily as any well-cared for baby.

The old woman suffered from malignant boils, and obtained a sorcerer one morning to cast out the devil which possessed her.

This Christian scientist opened the performance by bashing a pair of cymbals together with unflagging energy, talking all the time, for rhetoric is the secret of nearly all such legerdemain. It was enough to make the deaf hear and the lame walk, but whether he cast any devils out of the hag, or not, I don't know, for he made such an outrageous noise that we were finally constrained to cast him out into the street.

Not however before he had made his lips so dry pronouncing spells, that the innkeeper had to cook him some meat and give him some wine, in addition to paying him a handsome fee for his fatuous offices!

Thus a month passed, and the new year approaching, we set out on 30th January for Hanchong-fu, distant eight stages. Before leaving we made presents to our friends at the doorway.

Each child received a cartridge case, a wooden box went to

one man, an empty tin to another, the entrails of a deer to the inn-keeper, till everybody beamed.

But the champion cup — an Odol bottle — was reserved for the wreck of a Taoist priest who occasionally visited us, and he nearly wrecked himself still more, bowing his thanks.

Doubtless future travellers through Ling-t'ai-miao will notice several foreign antiques in the rooms of native art connoisseurs.

For two entire days the trail over the mountains led through a gorge of exquisite beauty, the cliffs, covered with pine and bamboo, rising abruptly two or three thousand feet above the ice-choked stream, making a grand play of colours in the winter sunshine.

At one time alongside the frothing torrent, at another giving precarious foothold up amongst the bush-clad precipices which yet towered far above, the trail wheeled sharply round bend after bend as it followed the sinuous curves of the river, affording endless views of matchless beauty. Beyond the projecting cliff which dipped boldly into the racing green waters, framing the picture for a moment, one more peep into the kaleidoscopic scenery always awaited us. A tiny white temple nestling amongst the dark pines which clothed a tongue of land, a glowing ochre scarp, several hundred feet high, crowned by waves of feathery bamboo; a sweep of firs hidden in a dark ravine, powdered with lingering snow that the dull warmth of winter had laid no hand on, all softened and blended in the mellow sunlight, and vignetted against the streak of twilit sky as night came on, ever changing in colour and in form.

Given facilities for travel, this gorge, the source of the Han river, one of the beauty spots of the world, would be the playground of China, rivalling as it does the Tyrol in majesty and the English Lakes in beauty.

On the third night an amusing incident occurred.

TAI-PEI-SAN

Before we reached our destination I became separated from the rest of the party, and darkness fell while I was still some distance behind.

Seeing nothing of them when I reached the village, I walked through the street out beyond the houses, and so back again, trying all the inns as I went, but without success; there were no white men there.

Finally I pushed open the door of a mule inn, determined that whatever happened, I would not spend the night outside when there was warmth so close at hand. It was dark inside, but by the glow of a charcoal fire I made out five mules stretched on the ground, and near the fire a bench, upon which I seated myself.

Becoming used to the gloom I now noticed for the first time a half imbecile wild-haired man facing me, disfigured by a big goitre, which caused him to gibber unintelligibly; but his patter drew a response from the next room where the innkeeper was in bed, and presently he came out and joined in the one-sided conversation.

The sight of a gun lying across my knees made the innkeeper rather nervous and taking a seat by the fire, he spoke in what might have been conciliatory tones; however it was no good as I did not understand him.

Next appeared the innkeeper's little boy, but he did not tend to enlighten the situation either, though he too joined glibly in the conversation.

At last the innkeeper, after a hurried consultation with his lieutenants, stretched across, and with a deprecating smile, put something into my hand.

It was ten cash!

Here was a comedy! a bribe of ten cash, or very nearly a farthing to go into the next street! And to soften the effect of his generous fiscal policy, the man pointed to his mouth and then at me, till it looked as if he was threatening to eat me.

At this I burst out laughing, which seemed to disconcert the innkeeper, who relapsed into silence.

Things were not shaping very rapidly. It seemed impossible to convince them of the peaceful nature of my mission, since the gesticulations I indulged in only served to scare them the more, it was very dull.

How I blamed a public school education which had not included Chinese in its curriculum!

At last, in the course of further conversation, up came the very word I wanted, the open-sesame of the situation. Tien-tsi! Yes, that was it, tien-tsi, an inn, and I soon made them understand that I was on the look-out for the inn. But to make one of them lead me there was another matter, and I steadfastly refused to go outside the door first. They might have shut me out!

Finally I coaxed the innkeeper with a charcoal brand in his hand as far as the door, and getting behind him, prodded him into the street with my gun; when he looked round he found a gun barrel eyeing him, and he had to go. It was a dismal scene. The imbecile sat on the bench, wringing his hands, the little boy stood by the door, wringing his eyes, and the highwayman drove his father away into the night.

So the old man led me over the cliff to the inn, which was barely a quarter of a mile away, the village being in two parts, and I rejoined the party, while the innkeeper fled back into the darkness.

On 5th February we reached the end of the gorge, and saw through the opening before us the plain of the upper Han; and next day we reached Hanchong-fu, eight hundred miles above Lao-ho-kow, the point where we had abandoned the Han three months previously.

5

The New Year

Hanchong-fu is a rather seedy looking city of about 70,000 inhabitants, and as in so many cities of western China, most of the business has been driven out by prohibitive likin duty, the best shops being situated in the east suburb.

The Han flows within a li of the east gate and is here a swift, shallow stream some sixty yards wide, though for a brief period during the summer rains it fills its bed, fully a quarter of a mile across.

The China Inland Mission has a station at Hanchong, and we spent several pleasant evenings with the missionaries; it was just over six weeks since we had seen white people. There are also Roman Catholics here, and the building easily mistaken for a prison is, strange to relate, the cathedral. The missionaries protest that the people are sufficiently amenable to spiritual amendment, but intensely averse to foreign interference, which aims at merely carnal amelioration, such as the projected railway down into Szechwan.

The plain of the upper Han is two thousand feet above sea level, and cursed for three quarters of the year with a sun which refuses to shine visibly, and though the mountains bound it so closely on either hand and converge rapidly upon Mien-hsien, only thirty miles to the west, it is a depressing locality.

ON THE ROAD TO TIBET

We occupied comfortable quarters at an inn situated on the Fu-kai, so that we found ourselves in the very vortex of the new year celebrations, to say nothing of the link-man, who shuffled by every half hour after sunset, hitting harmony out of a gong in order to warn intending burglars to suspend operations for a minute or two till he had gone past.

The official explanation which underlies this objectionable practice centres round the idea that it prevents people from falling too sound asleep, thus keeping them ever on the qui vive as to the safety of their own property. But however economical in policemen, the altruistic action of the watch in prohibiting people from indulging in sound slumber, even for their own ultimate benefit, is liable to be misconstrued by the weary traveller.

Certainly at night the street looked very picturesque, with its rows of swollen lanterns of all colours, dangling in front of the shops, and dancing to the evening breeze. It was sufficiently light now to make out what it was you tripped over in the dark.

On 15th February we set out for Tow-chow-ting, distant eighteen stages, taking the direct route through Mien-hsien, the most westernly city in Shensi destroyed by the T'ai-pings, now little more than a name with a few buildings to mark its site, and Lio-yang.

This latter city stands on the broad and rapid Kia-ling river, which empties itself into the Yangtze at Chung-king. The Kia-ling, though an inconsiderable tributary of the Yangtze, which it enters 1,500 miles from the sea, is navigable for some distance above Lio-yang, right down to Chung-king, about 700 miles distant, and it is facts like these which more than anything else, impress us with the magnificence of the Yangtze waterway.

We crossed the river by ferry in a bitterly cold north wind, the refractory mules as usual giving a lot of trouble getting into the scow. Two days later we struck the Kia-ling again at a big

THE NEW YEAR

bend, and we had cause to remember the day, as one of the mules slipped on the mountain path and sent his load over the edge into the river bed, luckily dry at that point; the damage was chiefly in enamel, but there was a spoon and a few other articles missing that evening.

Whether or not the fact is to be attributed to the influence of the Buddhist religion (however distorted), life in China is contemplated through such pessimistic spectacles, indeed as such a serious matter that, even amongst the wealthy, to devote time to the amusement of children is not considered a worthy cause; nor are the children sufficiently enterprising to devise amusements for them- selves.

Consequently toys, games, and other innocent diversions amongst the young are rarely met with, and if the child is father to the man one need never look for anything romantic in the latter since there was never any "make-believe" in the former.

True, one meets babies decked out with many an ornamental bauble, but the muleteer does as much for his mules, and such embellishments, it is understood, are not for the edification of the recipient.

The new year however serves as an excuse for several departures from stereotyped life, and marks also the great annual distribution of presents, a function which is religiously gone through with grave mockery.

The presents, chiefly in the form of cakes, poultry, pickled eggs and other delicate indigestibles, are lavished first upon the highest officials, and these gentlemen having set aside a small portion of the vast accumulation due to their rank, shuffle the remainder thoroughly and deal them out amongst the lesser officials from whom they came in the first place.

These lesser officials then proceed in a similar manner with the next substratum of the population, and so on till every one looks sleek and satisfied. But as usual it is the peasants who dance to the mandarin pipes in the end, for by the time we get back to them it is long odds on their getting anything at all!

At this season too every child possesses a ding-dong. This consists of a glass bulb flattened on one side and drawn out into a stem on the other, the flat bottom being made very thin and flexible, so that by alternately sucking and blowing into the stem it jerks backwards and forwards with a sharp clicking sound.

These simple toys are made in Hsianfu, and in Hanchong-fu cost two cash each. That is to say, after being carried by coolies three hundred miles over the mountains, about fourteen days' journey, they are sold at the equivalent rate of five for a farthing.

Chinese children seem to be neither original nor energetic, and the only other amusements we noticed them indulge in were kite-flying and swinging. Every village now had its swings, and in the evening they were always the centre of a crowd of boys of all ages, awaiting their turn; but this pastime does not survive the first month.

A curious and picturesque custom prevails in this part of the country, the people decorating their doorways with big branches of evergreens or even with entire trees, planted just outside; little strips of white paper, like small flags, are sometimes attached to the branches, and the combined effect of a number of such new year trees lining both sides of a village street is decidedly pleasing, reminding us somewhat of our own Christmas trees.

In Kansu we were at once greeted by severe snow storms, nor was the scenery, even under such a spotless mantle, impressive, for the mountains here consist entirely of loess and sedimentary rocks, shales, conglomerates and sandstones, often sufficiently iron stained to give a prevailing red tint to the soil. Interstratified with the soft shales and clays, great bands of harder limestone can frequently be traced right cross a mountain face, and the

THE NEW YEAR

prevalence of such hard sills gave origin to numerous cascades in the streams. The peaks were for the most part of inconsiderable altitude, flat topped, and cultivated to their summits, and altogether the scenery of south eastern Kansu was of a totally different stamp to anything we had yet seen; from the point of view of the naturalist at least the almost complete absence of trees and undergrowth made it as barren as a desert.

Meanwhile festivities were gathering in volume and intensity each night, the people were growing correspondingly hilarious, and everything was working up for the culmination of the year's frivolity with the feast of lanterns on the fifteenth of the month. That was a warlike night. The street was ablaze with lanterns of quaint design and rich colouring, and every door was thrown wide permitting a glimpse of the altar to the household god, supported by as many candles as there was room for; and from darkness till sunrise drums were rolling, cymbals clashing, and strings of crackers going off with a sound like the rattle of musketry.

On the last day of February we crossed the main watershed in a blinding snowstorm at an altitude of 9,000 feet and dropped down the valley to Ma-wu situated in a country of metamorphic rocks and raw hillsides framing a district by no means so dismal as Kansu had presented itself to us hitherto; and here we stayed long enough to shoot a good series of small deer which were abundant on the grassy mountain tops.

We were now in a rich grazing country and with the melting of the snow in the middle of March the brown hillsides were soon speckled with flocks and ringing with the melodious tinkle of cattle bells. All day long bright-eyed dirty-faced children basked in the sunshine amongst the rocks, warmly clad in spite of their bare legs, for these swarthy sons of Pan were clothed in long white felt coats, pressed into shape without stitch or seam, from a single mass of wool.

After leaving Ma-wu, the road traversed an extremely desolate and sparsely populated country of wild valleys, culminating at an altitude of about ten thousand feet on the grass plateau, where the snow still lay thick in the sheltered hollows and on the slopes of the mountains which ringed it in. Here another of those incidents inseparable from travel in China delayed us, and at the same time illustrated a possible side of the Chinese character which happily we rarely had to complain of.

Amongst the intricate glens and passes leading up to the plateau, we missed the road, and by the time we had regained it, dusk was rapidly falling, though we were still a long way from our destination.

At nightfall we passed through a small village, and stopping to make some enquiries about the road, were informed by one man that our mules had gone through earlier; whereupon we pushed ahead in the dark. Unfortunately Liuchin, which marked the end of our stage, was off the road, and to have attempted crossing the plateau in the darkness, seamed as it was with deep water-courses and bogs, in the hope of striking a small village the exact locality of which we did not know, would have been sheer folly.

Consequently, when in the neighbourhood of our destination. we set about knocking up the inmate of a lonely mill, requesting him to guide us through the intricacies of the plateau, the remaining distance to Liu-chin.

A long delay now ensued before this unfortunate native would consent to leave his stronghold, the door of which resounded with blows, and when at last he appeared, he was nearly scared out of his wits, and trembling in every limb.

To be roused from slumber at nine o'clock on a winter night in order to lead three white men across the moor is not, perhaps,

THE NEW YEAR

a common experience for a Chinaman in the wilds of Kansu, and even the promise of an adequate reward is hardly sufficient to allay his fears of immediate violence.

However, soothing words had their reward, and our guide, having first procured a torch, was soon picking his way rapidly across country to Liu-chin, we following hard at his heels as best we might.

The village proved to be only a quarter of a mile distant from the road, but concealed behind the shoulder of a low hill, so that we might easily have wandered half the night without coming upon it, for a Chinese village shows no lights after dark.

But a bitter disappointment was in store for us, and the hot meal and warm blankets so sorely needed after thirteen hours' continuous tramping, were not forthcoming; the mules had not arrived after all!

It was nearly ten o'clock when, after some difficulty, we gained admittance to an inn and made out, as best we could, on what the innkeeper willingly prepared for us — some hot tea and a basin of mien, taken, seated on the k'ang deck-boards, under which a few lumps of smouldering peat produced a faint warmth.

Desperately cold and miserable as we were, however, weariness would not be denied, and the long night was relieved by a few snatches of sleep.

So day broke, and though breakfasting on the humble fare of the inn and again resigning ourselves to patient waiting, yet no mules came.

This is what had happened.

By the time the slow moving mules had reached the plateau, it was already dark and on this bleak waste of grassland, unrelieved by tree or rock, the road, never conspicuous by day, was absolutely indistinguishable by night — as we had reason to know.

Amongst the streams and bogs, men and animals now floundered, straying hopelessly, and it was eleven o'clock when they at length reached the village previously referred to, where we had obtained news of them.

Doubtless they were now in no condition to push on another six or seven miles in any case, but enquiry at various inns elicited the information that no white men had passed through!

Yet we had stood there some minutes in conversation with half a dozen men, seen of many, and the fact that white men had been through must have been known by the greater part of the village.

In the face of this evidence, however, the muleteers could only stop and await our arrival, nor could they account for our delay.

See how small consequences are fraught with great results.

On the previous evening Dr. Smith had had occasion to remonstrate with a small boy for shouting after us in the street, and during the course of the morning the head muleteer, who had again made enquiries for us all over the village without result, by chance overheard the small boy relating the incident to a friend, from which he rightly enough concluded that we had actually come through on the previous day, a fact which had presumably been suppressed by the innkeeper and his friends, for the sake of profit.

Whereupon breakfast, which had been prepared against our expected arrival, was packed up, and the mules hurried to our relief, arriving with much needed comforts soon after mid-day.

On this plateau, now covered with a scanty growth of brown grass, peat was dug from many of the marshy hollows and burned for fuel; there was nothing else.

Possibly this region is another of the great grass plateau, to be referred to later, which begins northwest of Towchow, isolated by the scooping out of the deep Tow valley. Our approach to the border was now made evident by the wooden p'ai-lou covered with Tibetan inscriptions and extravagant paintings of conventional Buddhas, which frequently spanned the road, and by the half-bred draught yak which pulled extraordinary looking carts, put together without the aid of a single piece of metal. In shape these latter were like our ordinary farm-yard carts at home, their most interesting feature being the wheels, which, besides having the form of irregular elipses, always strayed into the third dimension, instead of being satisfied with two, as a well behaved wheel should.

The rims were usually made up of two semi-circles, or what purported to be semi-circles, bent from birch saplings, and dove-tailed together; but not infrequently six arcs, similarly fitting into each other, were employed.

It made one's eyes ache to stand behind and watch these wheels wobbling along in complicated spirals, to the dismal clanking of a great iron bell swinging from the axle.

On 17th March we reached Min-chow, a small city situated where three valleys meet at an elevation of 8,000 feet on the south bank of the Tow river.

In appearance it is even more dilapidated than Hanchong, seemingly not having been altogether tidied up since the Mohammedan rebellion, fifty years ago. Inside the city there is nothing whatever to see, and, as usual, the business is done outside, in the south and east suburbs.

To complete its woe-begone appearance the practice of digging the mud with which to build the houses, in situ, has so lowered the general level inside the wall beneath that of the surrounding valley floor, that in wet weather the city becomes a sort of artesian well or sump, and resembles a gigantic mud-wallow.

ON THE ROAD TO TIBET

The only knoll in the morass is occupied by the mission station, which commands a view over the whole city; and this piece of land was given by the inhabitants themselves.

To us weary travellers who had seen no white faces for nearly five weeks, Mr. Eckvall, of the Evangelical Mission, was hospitality itself, but we were unable to spend as much time in Min-chow as we should have liked.

Two days after our arrival, therefore, we struck the Tow river, and, ascending the valley, entered the Tibet border country.

6

THE TIBET BORDER

Two days' tramp brought us to Choni, a walled village of considerable importance though of mean appearance, situated on the north bank of the Tow river in a mountain alcove. Here we were welcomed by Mr. and Mrs. Christie, whose work lay amongst the Tibetans, and these hospitable missionaries spared no pains to make us comfortable and to further our interests.

Choni, the capital of a considerable district in Amdoa which is Chinese territory in name only, is inhabited chiefly by Tibetans, and is a hotbed of Lamaism, carrying on a sort of guerilla warfare with the mission over the souls of the local agnostics. It means not only social extinction for a Tibetan to be converted, but also implies that the proselyte must fly for his life, and the several exiled Christian natives living on the mission premises testified to the thoroughness of a work which provides for those whose spiritual welfare is purchased at the expense of bodily damnation.

Mr. Christie was however known and respected by these wild Tibetans even though they refused to forsake mammon, and his influence extended widely amongst them in social matters.

Nevertheless one could well understand that it would be easier to evangelize a Tibetan with a blunderbuss than with a hymn-book, and the work of fifteen years in these regions has born little fruits though that which has ripened is of the Garden of Hesperides.

The persecution to which some Christians had been subjected recalls the days of the Inquisition, and hounded from their homes, their cattle and land confiscated, threatened with torture and death did they not recant, they had nowhere to flee but to those who had weaned them from their degradation.

Worst of all is it for a priest to renounce his faith, for the monastery in this priest-ridden land is omnipotent; at least one male in every family is sacrificed to a monastery and to forsake Lamaism is as it were to betray King, country and religion all at once, and go over to the enemy.

Realising that it is impossible for a Christian Tibetan to remain in his home, the mission have recently purchased a disused temple on the banks of the Tow, and in this secluded retreat these poor outcasts will in future find a haven of refuge, to live their lives in peace away from the petty intrigues of their scheming countrymen.

The mission house at Choni had a romantic history, besides being haunted.

Some sixty years ago it sheltered a Regent of Tibet, during that period when a succession of Dalai Lamas (to the malignant satisfaction of China) were unable to survive the tender age of eighteen.

On this functionary's return from Lhasa on one occasion, the joyous people of Choni made welcome with crackers and torchlight processions, and enthusiasm for illumination waxed so high that they finally made a bonfire of the Regent's house itself — quite by accident of course.

To atone for their zeal they rebuilt the house with the very best materials that the countryside produced — the very stoutest timber and the very nicest mud.

THE TIBET BORDER

Some years later, after the Regent had passed away, the skeleton of a Tibetan was found in one of the lower rooms, the rats having run off with the rest of him. Consequently the house was shunned for ever afterwards till the mission bought it some years ago.

We slept soundly and never noticed any ghost ourselves but if there had been one, we should have smelt him coming long before he arrived, for the Tibetans are perfectly poisonous people within a range of a hundred yards up wind, and ghosts sufficiently material to affect the optic nerve may bo expected to affect that of smell also. Many of the princes of eastern Tibet reside in the border country, and of these the most powerful is the Prince of Choni, despot of 75,000 Tibetans, divided into forty-eight clans, well versed in the art of robbery under arms. Not a few of these turbulent Lamaists live by relieving travellers of their superfluous goods, and now that they have by such means made their territory secure from invasion, they continue to relieve one another in the same way. Some of the clans, however, are peaceful tillers of the soil and others are nomads.

They pay annual tribute to their Prince in money or in kind. Sycee, flocks, grain or even in raw gold dust, but a temple perched on a cliff near Choni reminds us that from time to time there have been murmurs of dissent; for this temple was built by a former prince to curse seven rebellious tribes up the river.

Shortly after our arrival in Choni, we paid a visit to the potentate, and having sent up our cards, stood waiting for some minutes in the courtyard of the yamen, surrounded by a little knot of curious retainers and underlings, parasites which infest every yamen.

At last, the prince having dressed, we were ushered into the state guest-room, to be immediately dazzled by cut glass and a lurid glow of embroidery shining from the walls, from the cushions, from the hanging lamps, from everything in fact that could possibly be embroidered. Even this splendour, startling as it was, was soon put in the shade however, for presently the Prince himself slid in like a perambulating sunset, a crimson silk ma-kua and and metallic-blue plush gown with gold brocade and buttons giving him the appearance of having recently stepped out of a band-box.

We ourselves were attired more in the garb of the remote mountains than of courtly ambassadors, and the mantle of shabbiness was in no way lightened by the gorgeous finery of this neurotic young man; nor did his obsequious mien and agricultural manner bias us in his favour.

He was of anaemic complexion, tall, thin, and were it not for the air of dissipation which shrouded him like an evil cloud, handsome. As it was, a peevish lad with more wives than babies, and a preference for smoking opium which necessitated his beginning the day with lunch. After the usual preliminaries of etiquette, and a basin of tea to wash down the taste, he brought out his rifle for cheap repairs—a mauser pattern, rather passe, informing us with an injured air that it would not work.

As we all found ourselves unable to pull back the bolt to open the breach, this was not surprising, but the Prince hastily declared that that was not the trouble at all, since the breach could easily be opened; and having set the butt on the floor he stepped boldy on the bolt, whereupon it rolled slowly back with a sound like the creaking of a rusty door, Dr. Smith recommended oil.

Perched on the hillside just beyond the village was the lamasery, with a complement of five hundred resident priests, the finest monastery in the Choni territory, which by the way, was about as large as Scotland.

Round the inside of the wall, which enclosed an area as large as the village itself, were ranged the little flat roofed dwellings

THE TIBET BORDER

of the priests, the centre being occupied by several temples and the throne rooms of the three living Buddhas, one of whom was only a little boy, reincarnation of a defunct lama who had only recently transmigrated. The chief temple was a magnificent building glowing with paints and whitewash, the roof ablaze with gold and bronze images.

At the top of a low flight of steps by which the entrance was approached were two rows of gaudy prayer wheels flanking the doors, and in the middle, a good sized hole, eroded by the devout supplicants tapping their heads on the stone when prostrating themselves before the temple.

I found the priests rather overwhelming. A Tibetan begins to perceptibly outrage one's olfactory sense at about the age of ten, and continues to do so till he dies, growing mellower all the time. No self-respecting native of eastern Tibet ever changes his clothes, and he has a perfect horror of soap only paralleled by his antipathy to water. They are not a prepossessing set, these priests, and very few of them, even judged by their own accommodating standards of righteousness, are sufficiently worthy to attain to the dignity of lama, the most eminent position to which a lama-priest can aspire in his first life.

Lamaism, like other forms of Buddhistic worship, imposes celibacy, abstinence, and other vicious virtues on its devotees, and it is safe to assume that when an exclusive body of men thus arrogate to themselves restraints more than human, they will end by sinking even beneath frailty, as most certainly do the majority of these debauched ecclesiastics.

The dignity of lama, with the chance of reincarnation, is conferred as the reward of blameless anti devoted life, yet there were fewer than a hundred lamas amongst these five hundred priests.

Their ignorance was appalling: few could read or write,

and of outside affairs they knew nothing. Nor had they great opportunities for improving their minds, since the only literature in the monastery consisted of the Buddhist scriptures with the Commentary, these being in fact almost the only words in Tibetan extant.

However, these alone, comprising 203 large volumes, would fill a small library, one volume being as much as a man can carry in his hands and a good deal more than he can carry in his head.

The hypocrisy practiced in divination scarcely merits the term fraud, since everyone is privy to the secret, and the function would be only ludicrous were it not so closely bound up with all that is solemn in the Lama religion.

After the death of a lama, or of an already reincarnated Buddlia, a babe (who must of course have been born since the death referred to, though it does not signify how long after) is divined to be his reincarnation, and it usually happens that he is born to a family whither the dead man had previously enjoined his sycophants to seek his reincarnation.

When the cliild is some months old the examination takes place.

To acquit himself creditably, he must recognise several articles as belonging to his former self, and this he invariably does to the complete satisfaction of everyone. It is a remarkable coincidence that the reincarnation discovered in this way always comes of a rich family, who, be it whispered, are always considerably poorer after the happy event.

If the reincarnation is that of a lama, he becomes in his second life a living Buddha; and a living Buddha may go on being reincarnated till he has spent thirteen lives; which is giving points to a cat.

Of course the child is secretly well primed beforehand, and there is money under the table, as the Tibetans say. The temple courts were crowded with these good priests trotting aimlessly about, pulling beads and twirling prayer wheels, at the same time muttering the everlasting prayer: Om! mani padme hum."

The efficacy of that little prayer, its antiseptic action on sin, is truly wonderful. The Lamaist who gets through it a few million times is a moral certainty of Nirvana whatever he does, and it is pathetic to see how hard the poor men work. London by night with its illuminated addresses informing you "Bovril" in yellow, which mysteriously disappears leaving you standing up stupidly at nothing, to notify you very slowly "Bovril" in red, and then suddenly change its mind in the most capricious manner and painfully spell "Odd" — London in this aggravating mood is skittles to a Tibetan monastery.

In order to facilitate to the utmost the accumulation of prayers by the above method, Lamaism as decreed that it is not necessary to say them; it is sufficient to see them, provided, apparently, that they are moving about.

Hence prayer wheels are on the move day and night grinding it out; prayer flags are fluttering day and night wafting it surreptitiously round the monastery, and every priest who can pull a bead is busy all day accumulating even by this comparatively sluggish process, thousands of it.

We have gone ahead ourselves in the way of mechanical contrivance; time is valuable, and we have devised many instruments to meet the trick it has of flying. But we have not yet got on quite so far that we are enabled to say our prayers by machinery.

A Tibetan proverb says: There is no sin so great as killing, an epigram worthy of a Delphi Oracle, for the natives of Amdoa are great offenders against the sixth commandment, though so exceptionally compassionate on the vermin which find sustenance on their persons.

But it is not to the oracular nature of the proverb that we need turn for an explanation of the inconsistency, but to the virtue of the rosary, the panacea of iniquity.

Murder is a sin, certainly, only to be exculpated by a large number of repetitions of the magic prayer, and flying to his rosary, the homicide has soon beaded his crime into the ewigkcit, to start afresh, with only half an hour lost to schedule time, in the race for Nirvana.

It is the cheapest form of assuaging conscience yet invented; even we with our vaunted progress have never devised anything half so plausible as that. But of course it makes killing rather cheap too.

At the lamasery we took tea with an old priest who had been in Lhasa when the British Mission entered the sacred city, a quiet, cheerful old man with pendent moustaches, and spectacles of ogre-like dimensions. Knowing the weakness of our stomachs he did not offer us Tibetan tea, which is seasoned with salt, the blackish fluid thus obtained supporting a lump of rancid butter to which wool is in the habit of adhering; but for all that it was as well not to scrutinize its hypercritically. From the ceiling of the low room hung meat, haunches of pork, slowly ripening. So little molestation had that pork undergone since the unfortunate pig's reincarnation that numerous spiders had found peace and repose for their delicate tapestry within its ample folds; and as far as we were able to judge they had no cause for, apprehension in the near future. A bountiful layer of floating particles had also effected a landing, and on the whole the pork looked pretty airtight. They did not offer us bacon however.

Being inside the lamasery taking photographs one morning, , the sound of priests chanting reached my ears, and on approaching the temple from which the sound proceeded, I found some hundreds of sandals lying about in heaps, and taking off my own boots, I entered the temple. It was nearly dark inside and the sombre gloom was accentuated by dozens of tiny butter lamps which burned like stars before the shrine of Buddha at the far end of the temple, and by a single shaft of sunlight which shot down from the centre of the lofty roof, touching with colour the strings of dingy prayer flags stretched across from side to side, and lighting up the massive pillars of the collonade. Seated cross-legged on strips of carpet, their soiled brown gowns pulled loosely over them, eight long rows of dusky figures stretched up to where the bloated living Buddhas, resplendent in red cloaks edged with faded yellow, sat on their thrones beneath the shadow of the golden image; and through the mystic twilight the chanting of two hundred priests came like some wild voice out of the night, rising and falling on the wind and echoing through the mountains.

Then all was still again, only one of the Buddhas was speaking in a hollow sepulchral voice, though the sound floated down easily enough; and again came the responses chanted by two hundred deep bass voices.

All of a sudden the chanting ceased, and the band crashed out, reverberating strangely through the wooden temple, the ringing jingle of the cymbals, the roll of drums, and mournful wailing of the conch-shells, like some dumb animal screaming with pain; a mad roar of sounds, contrasting oddly enough with the dirge-like praying of the priests.

This noise too ceased as suddenly as it had begun, and again the dark temple was filled with the swinging sound of men praying.

Presently someone struck a stone gong three times, and as the dull echo died away the chanting ceased.

Instantly a dozen priests entered bearing large buckets of wine and plates full of thin butter slabs, which they handed along the rows of dry mouthed supplicants, each of whom produced a wooden vessel from within the folds of his gown. The interval for refreshments had arrived.

It was all inexpressibly weird in that gloomy temple, with its dead and living gods, its flickering lights and shifting shadows, and its bursts of prayer and wild music, as I stood, the cynosure of every eye, listening with bated breath to the blare of the conchshells and the roll of drums, drinking in to the full the strange fascination of a pagan service.

The Tow river was some fifty yards across opposite Choni, running like a mile race, and frequently interrupted by rapids.

There was a wooden bridge a mile below the village, but a raft plied across just opposite to us; and on the other side of the river were the forested mountains of the fên-tsi territory.

Wishing to cross the river early one morning before many people were astir, I decided that, rather than walk right away down to the bridge, I would try and manipulate the raft and punt pole myself; I knew something of the queer evolutions of punts from experiences at Cambridge.

There had been a snowstorm in the night, and the cat-icc was grinding against the shingle along the river edge; the water looked gray and cold, and the snow hung in festoons from the fir trees. But that would all disappear when the sun got up.

Pushing off the raft, which was frozen to the shingle just out of reach of the water I jumped on board and seized the pole. Next second we were spinning down the river.

I jabbed the pole into the water, but it boggled in the rapid current, and I all but capsized; at the next attempt I spun the raft round in a circle, and before I knew what was happening, I was nearly a hundred yards below my starting point, in a rapid, and the waves were dashing over the floor boards.

The river here was divided by a narrow island of shingle, and

THE TIBET BORDER

we were racing down a narrow channel, almost within jumping distance of the island.

All aspirations of getting the raft ashore having vanished, I flung down the punt pole, and consigning the whole outfit to the river just above a heavy rapid, I sprang for the island, landed in shallow water, and paddled ashore, while my late craft sped along on its way to Minchow.

The channel which separated me from the mainland was deep and rapid; several attempts to wade it showed that it would be impossible from any point of the island. A broader but shallower channel separated me from the other side and to gain time, I continued my original journey, wading across the twenty yards which separated me from the further bank.

The water was well above my knees, and the current so strong that it was necessary to proceed extremely slowly, for once down, it would have been impossible to regain a footing.

Having crossed, and returned cautiously to my island however, I was as badly off as ever, and cast about me how I could cross the deep channel without tramping right down to the bridge.

I shivered at the thought, but there was nothing else for it, so having divested myself of a coat and sweater, I walked to the head of the island, so as to get across before I struck the big rapid at the lower end. As I plunged in and a wave came over me, I gasped, and thought I should never draw in another breath; the cold water was a dreadful shock.

A few strokes athwart the current and I was across, and landing some thirty yards below my starting point, surprised a whole heap of pretty Tibetan girls who had come down to wash their clothes. They had watched my preparation with no less amusement than astonishment, and probably could not understand anyone being mad enough to bathe in the icy Tow at that hour of the morning; but they did not understand how very unsought after the pleasure had been. So I trotted up to the mission house coatless, my clothes slowly freezing stiff; the raft was recovered about a mile down the river, and I decided to defer punting till the summer came.

From Choni we proceeded north westwards to Tow-chow, old city, fifteen miles distant, our host. on this occasion being Mr. Simpson, one of the earliest of the Tibet border pioneers. Tow-chow-ting, a small military post situated in a mountain depression, a few miles north of the Tow river, is 9000 feet above sea level, and enjoys a bracing climate.

The surrounding mountains, composed of a curious red sandstone or conglomerate, are quite bare of trees or scrub, and at this season supported no vegetation whatever, though the rows of terraces into which they were cut, proclaimed the fact that they were green in summer.

Tow-chow was built by the Mongols during the T'ang dynasty, about a thousand years ago, though for the past five hundred years it has been of no political importance, except as a frontier city.

Just across the Tow river, about five miles to the south,. are the ruins of a still older city, about which little is known, while Tow-chow new city, twenty miles to the west, is purely Chinese and of comparatively recent date. The population of the old city is chiefly Mohammedan, the magnificent mosque being, indeed, the only building of any interest; but there is a large floating population of Tibetans, and Mongols from the west and north, who come to bring skins to the market, Tow-chow being one of the greatest emporiums for furs in western China.

7

Amongst The Tibetans

During a month spent in these regions we undertook two hunting trips into the fen-tsi country, of which the Tow river and the edge of the great plateau may be considered the boundaries.

The status quo of this territory, lying between Chinese Kansu and Tibet proper, is rather nebulous. Geographically, it is obviously enough part of Amdoa, outer Tibet, the Tow river forming the boundary as far west as Tow-chow, beyond which city the boundary turns northwards, following the edge of the grassland plateau, which is quite sharply defined.

But so considered, its political status is not made any clearer, since it does not come under the jurisdiction of the Amban at Sining, who controls the great Koko Nor province of which Amdoa is a part.

Actually, the various tribes inhabiting the fen-tsi country owe allegiance to their own hereditary princes who are rather more independent of the Dalai Lama than they are of the shadowy suzerain power at Peking, but the practice adopted in many maps of drawing an arbitrary division between outer Tibet and China ignores both geographical possibilities and political actualities, though it bolsters up the claim of Peking to extend her authority (still on paper) a little further west each year.

We proceeded first to a small village near the head of a long valley, some thirty miles south of Choni across the Tow river and over against the country of the Tepos, the most turbulent of the tribes.

Amongst the Tepos no Chinaman, be he official or trader, dare venture without a strong escort, and though, by going due south from Tow-chow over the mighty Pei-ling range, Sung-pan may be reached in eight days, the journey is rarely made. Mules cannot be taken across, so that the slow moving yak transport must be employed. A wonderful view of these mountains is obtained from the heights above Tow-chow, and the pass fifty miles distant is clearly seen, an extraordinary sight. This pass, or stone gate as it is called, is a deep sword-cut in the mountains, a wedge of rock having apparently been cut out of the range to a depth of several thousand feet, the narrow road being thus flanked by two stupendous buttresses which, though not quite sheer, do not in any part of their height diverge more than 30° from the perpendicular.

The illusion of the stone gate is lost when one reaches the spot however, for the two cliffs are in reality ten or twelve miles apart, a conclusion one would never arrive at viewing them from Tow-chow owing to the very pronounced foreshortening.

The Pei-ling range itself is so tremendously steep and craggy that though the peaks rise to between eighteen and twenty thousand feet, immense screes and gullies of bare rock are exposed amidst the eternal snow. The Chinese government has sent troops a short distance into this territory more than once, but never with success, and the grim humour with which these expeditions were treated is really delightful. On one occasion having stolen the entire baggage train, they finally stole the very horse which the chen-tai himself rode! — but it needs a Chinaman to fully appreciate the humiliating position of the poor military official who had to walk back to Tow-chow and explain his inglorious case.

Later, a squad of cavalry fared no better, all their animals being stolen by these ingenious filchers during the night. On hearing of this outrage, some responsible official sent a bombastic message to the Tepo chief, intimating that if the animals were not restored at once things really would happen; whereupon the horses were sent back to the Chinese camp. But alas, when they arrived, all the tails were found to have been bobbed by the jokers.

This village to which we repaired then was a mere handful of flat- roofed houses situated at an altitude of nearly eleven thousand feet, and on learning the object of our visit, a friendly hunter at once put at our disposal the best room in his house (which happened to be the kitchen), and we made ourselves very comfortable camping on the floor.

Our neighbours were pleasant and friendly. The Tibetans exhibit none of that vulgar curiosity which is the bane of the rural Chinese, and their somewhat haughty indifference to all things which concerned us was a great relief after the microscopic scrutiny to which we had been subjected for so long.

Though in personal cleanliness the Tibetan yields even to the Chinaman, yet their houses are vastly superior, being roomy and scrupulously clean.

On an article of furniture which is I believe called a dresser were ranged china bowls like so much old porcelain, and well polished brass vessels, giving quite an air of refinement to the kitchen, and it was delightful to see the housewife actually go round the room each morning dusting the walls and household goods — on to our beds. A long mud cooking range, in one end of which was sunk a huge copper, and a low k'ang completed the furnishing of the apartment.

Moreover so rigid was the etiquette of the establishment that we were not permitted to whistle inside the house, for the

Tibetans believe that to do so invites disaster.

This mountain village could not have mustered fifty people all told, and the men were chiefly hunters, woodsmen and herdsmen; the people are too indolent, too tolerant of a hand-to-mouth existence, to cultivate more than the barest amount that would suffice, and the women were responsible for most of that; but excellent fresh milk could be bought here, a luxury unknown in China.

The men are frequently handsome, tall and slim, but even these peaceful villagers are apt to exhibit a hardness in the lines of the face which betrays them as belonging to a ruthlessly cruel people. The women too are comely, far more than the Chinese, at least when young, and their well knit figures, undeformed feet and breezy, unrestrained bearing betoken a more exalted social standing than is allowed to their less fortunate sisters. But the strenuous life and rigorous climate age them prematurely.

The scenery amidst which we were now placed was magnificent.

All around us rose the mountains, densely clothed on their shaded slopes with silver and spruce fir, giving place in the warmer hollows to masses of willow showing as brilliant patches of purple and ochre amongst the olive green of the sombre forest.

In the morning the graceful tops of these dark trees were always powdered with fresh fallen snow, and as the sun rose into the brilliant sky, they glowed and sparkled with the charm of a thousand Christmas trees.

Behind them, immense pinnacles of yellow limestone, flashing in the sunlight, reared themselves far above the forests, their sharp summits, where the eagles nest pricking through the soft snow mists which wrap them round and writhe to and fro as the wind rockets through the scree-fed gullies.

Far below in the deeply graven valley the stream went

singing over the boulders between its ice walled banks, bursting through gorge beyond gorge where the arching trees almost met overhead, leaving the jagged rent, through which the confused waters splashed heavily from one deep green pool to another, dark and noisy.

In one place the bald cliffs, here hewn into fantastic pillars and impregnable battlements on which even the clinging snow flakes find no rest, rose upwards till the roar of the torrent was drowned in the clouds; in another place the snow lay deep in the shadow of the fir-clad hills which sloped back tier beyond tier till the river was lost to view behind the forest barrier.

But no temples crown these lonely mountains as in China; no prosperous villages cluster in the sequestered valleys, no cultivated terraces chequer the slopes; only here and there a prayer-wheel stands stark and mute, strangled in the iron grip of the ice. There are no green leaves yet, no bursting buds breaking into joyful life, no flowers, though this is April, the sun shining brilliantly in a clear sky, the birds singing merrily in the copses.

For out here on the grass hills above the forest, where the dead haulms of a thousand decayed flowers are still splitting and cracking in the snow, we are fifteen thousand feet above the sea.

In these wilds we hunted the precipice sheep, a beast that settles on top of a rock like a church steeple and looks disdainfully round at the landscape (with figures in the foreground) as though he would sing: —

Odi profanum vulgus, Et arceo.

The chief occupation of the figures in the foreground was to climb grimly up one side of a precipice on all fours and shoot cheerfully down the other, all sixes and sevens, taking in unsolicited mouthfuls of rock and snow en route.

It was prodigious. So thin was the air in these regions that after wheezing like a leaky cylinder till I was blue in the face, I was compelled to sit down every hundred yards and inflate myself at leisure, lest chronic puncture set in. With the sweat pouring from our faces, we plunged knee deep through the snow, our feet too cold to feel pain and only a dull aching sensation telling us that something was still there, till by lying on our backs and looking up towards the sky we saw several precipice-sheep; once indeed we saw a whole bunch of them, but they were a good distance off — several miles I should say.

Of course we were always at a disadvantage when chasing these frolicsome creatures because we had to haul guns along; they hadn't. The feeling stole over me many a time that I could have laid mine gently down in the snow and abandoned it without the slightest compunction only it might have made the sheep smile. Anyhow we pursued those sheep up amongst the clouds for three days and they had the laugh every time: all they had to think of was holding on; all we had to think of was not letting go, and at the end of those three days the boy scouts might have tracked us all over the mountains by means of the pieces of clothing and morsels of flesh we left hooked on to the rocks during a bright but brief passage. But never a baa-lamb did we slay.

Leaving the village we now descended to a lower valley and spent a couple of nights in a deserted hunter's hut, built of rough logs roofed with birch bark, and situated near the haunts of the ma-lo or big horse-deer of the Tibet border.

We saw several of these fine beasts, but being much hunted on account of their horns which are exported for medicine, they are extremely wild and far too wary for anyone but a skilled hunter.

Though still at a considerable altitude we found camping out pleasant enough now, and the nights warmer than might have been expected considering that snow still fell; but lack of provisions soon forced us to return to Choni.

Our next expedition was out on to the grass plateau, thirty miles north-west of Tow-chow, and here we found rude quarters in a small village at an altitude of 12,000 feet. The contrast in the surroundings of the two places could hardly have been more pronounced.

In place of majestic crags and precipices, the undulating hills of the plateau; in place of the dark needle-leaved forest, the barren grass of limitless prairie with never a tree as far as the eye could reach; in place of the mountain torrent, the discoloured half frozen stream winding sluggishly down the hollows. Desolation and bleakness and biting cold hung over all the plateau, over the dead brown vegetation but a few inches high which clothed it like an insufficient garment, over the bare gray granite boulders which capped the lifeless hilltops where not even grass would grow, over the stagnant black marshes between, extending even to the distant peaks away to the south, streaked and freckled with eternal snow.

Through these inhospitable regions roamed great herds of sheep, yak and shaggy ponies, the care of the nomadic herdsmen whose rude skin tents, dark in colour and square in shape, occupied sheltered nooks in the shallow valleys. A few miserable villages there were too, scattered, far apart, and out of the driving snowstorms sweeping incessantly over the grass hills, pale white walls would suddenly appear, to finally take shape as a lonely lamasery.

There was no cultivation; the only fuel was the dung of the animals which found a wretched sustenance on these wastes, and the acrid smoke from this smouldering offal filled every tent and hut.

And yet for a few months in the year the plateau might look

even beautiful, rich with green grass and sparkling with flowers. But in April the time was not ripe when for a brief space life might venture forth; only the ground-hogs scampered about amongst their burrows, waving their stiff tails up and down like signal arms and uttering shrill whistles like an express train; and herds of antelope, matching the russet sward so closely in colour as to be almost invisible, wandered over the hills.

The few people met with on the lonely plateau are not entirely reassuring in appearance, and the only mule train I saw crossing the hills was accompanied by an armed escort.

Further in the interior, where only nomadic tribes wander from place to place, almost all men are robbers when occasion arises; but here were scattered villages and monasteries, and nomadic herdsmen carrying on an intermittent trade with the city.

Nevertheless every man, even to the meanest priest, carries a sword buckled round his waist, and the solitary horseman, magnificent in sheepskin coat edged with leopard fur and fox skin cap, occasionally encountered cantering across country on his own or someone else's pony, as though about to swoop hawk-like on some unsuspecting prey, always has his long gun slung behind.

But it was the priests from the solitary lamaseries who were the most ferocious looking scoundrels I have ever seen, their piercing black eyes looking out from swarthy faces seemingly blotched with every evil passion and half satisfied lust which the wit of devil could offer them.

It had taken us nearly twelve hours' tramp to reach our destination, of which rather more than half had been across the grass hills after attaining the plateau a couple of thousand feet above Tow-chow.

Imagine a country absolutely devoid of landmarks, a

monotonous expanse of rolling brown hills, the same view greeting the eye whether one turned to north or south, to east or west, unless, indeed a sweep of snow-clad peaks on the horizon may be considered to constitute a guide as to direction. It was as the open sea, and to steer a course a compass was required, though under favourable conditions the sun or stars above might have been relied on.

Shortly after we had settled down on the grass hills, I left the party a couple more days hunting and set out alone for Towchow confident of following the route we had previously taken and of reaching the city by nightfall. It was a brighter day than usual and from time to time the sun showed up, allowing a little warmth to creep over the frozen plateau.

For a couple of hours all went well; the trail was conspicuous enough, while a granite tor here, a stream or gully there, recalled the route to mind. The first and indeed the fatal interruption was the result of a sudden invasion of the premises by three mastiffs from out of a nomad's tent close at hand.

Tibetan mastiffs need to be taken seriously. They are large of limb and ruthless of purpose, possessing that great virtue so rarely seen in domestic animals, the power of concerted action. They think nothing of springing on the intruder, and never take leave without taking something else too even if it is only a portion of one's clothing; the asking of questions comes later. Accordingly I proceeded cautiously and kept a severe eye on them till they had seen me safely off the estate.

By the time this unwelcome espionage had been removed I would seem to have been badly side-tracked, though it was an hour later that I discovered the fact, in contemplating a large and unfamiliar lamasery from the depths of which issued, like the trickle of muddy water, a file of dirty priests.

Having made this ugly observation I left the trail altogether and endeavoured to make my way in an easterly direction in the hope of rejoining the lost road; but being ignorant of the time, apparently found the sun a fickle goddess.

In this way I picked up several more trails, mere sheep walks, yet matters proceeded from bad to worse and by the middle of the afternoon I was forced to confess myself inextricably mixed and wandering more or less at random amongst the endless grass hills, looking for the elusive edge of the plateau with no very definite idea in which direction it lay.

From time to time I met men, herdsmen for the most part, but as none of them understood a word of Chinese, even Tow-chow being known by a different name amongst the Tibetans, they were unable to help me had they been so inclined. Once indeed towards evening I encountered some wild looking horsemen who shouted to me and approached inconveniently near, while I, with my eyes on them, edged warily away keeping one hand in my pocket where reposed a Colt pistol, cocked and loaded. It might have proved a disastrous tribunal to which to appeal in a hostile country, but anyhow it should be the final one, and I felt more secure with its friendly presence; on the other hand the intentions of these men, though couched in such uncompromising terms, might have been entirely friendly. Nevertheless it was with a sigh of relief that I saw the unknown characters turn off at a tangent and gallop away, talking and laughing.

It was now nearing sunset, and as if to leave a good impression lingering, the sky, which had been overcast suddenly cleared, and the sun blazed over the western mountains; but it was humiliating to discover that for some hours at least while wandering aimlessly I had been travelling almost duo westwards. Now Tow-chow lay south-east.

At that moment, while rounding the shoulder of a low hill, I saw over the rise the tops of several strange black shapes, ground hogs as I supposed on reflection after a momentary start, when, stepping forward I saw, not ground hogs, but six or eight kites which at once flew up, but apprehending no danger, continued to hover like sullen ghouls round the spot, loth to leave in spite of my unwelcome appearance.

Turning the corner I found myself face to face with their ghastly repast.

It was a baby boy, probably not more than two months old, stretched naked on the ground, a raw wound where the kites had fed in the lower part of the trunk.

There was no reason to suspect infanticide. The Tibetans dispose of their dead either by casting them thus to the carrion or by throwing them to the fish of the river; yet the eyes widely open, staring, glazed in death, the arms outstretched and slightly raised as though to clasp a mother's neck, the lips parted as though to cry out and thus transfixed with the cry still unuttered — these things looked horrible in the gathering dusk of that desolate place and I hurried on, conscious of a sudden drop in my spirits. Night was coming on, and shortly afterwards, striking a long valley which led southwards, I started down it, anything being preferable to that awful plateau.

It was some hours after dark when I stopped, many miles down the valley, unable to pick my way in safety any longer; yet there were seven hours at least before dawn, and in a very restless frame of mind I sat down under a rock, my eyes strained to the east. Little clusters of flat-roofed mud houses, like piles of children's bricks scattered here and there had already shown me that I was leaving the plateau behind, but beyond the fact that I was now travelling approximately south towards the Tow river, I knew nothing.

I felt tired now, and hungry, for since an early breakfast I had only eaten a small piece of bread; but the little piece remaining I felt must be kept in reserve so I took only a mouthful for supper. To make matters worse it began to snow and shift as I would in the inky darkness it was impossible to find shelter from the cold wet wind which blustered up the valley.

Throughout the night I reviewed the position in all its bearings. There could no longer be any doubt that I had come much too far west, possibly also too far south, and that on the morrow I must travel eastwards in order to reach the city. So eased in mind I anxiously awaited the leaden-winged dawn.

Before the east was gray I set out down the valley, and picking up a trail across the stream with daylight, struck eastwards.

Past several vast monasteries, their pale white walls and golden roofs shining dimly through the morning mist, and sometimes a collection of shepherd huts I went, thankful to see signs of habitation again; and so up hill and down dell. But still, though there were hills and valleys it was desolate and wild, and Tibetans, solitary and suspicious looking, were as rare as on the previous day.

It was a cruel day, and before I had crossed three valleys it was snowing heavily and colder than ever; moreover in ascending a ridge I presently found myself, to my inexpressible disgust, enveloped in driving mist and, what was worse, on a trail which rapidly dwindled and lost itself in some more grass hills, nor could I see in front any valleys like those I had been crossing, only rolling plateau again as far as the eye could reach.

It was a mockery standing there with the driving snow slashing into my face, and the clammy mists coming and going, wrapping me as in a wet shroud; the outlook was worse than ever.

At that moment the fog lifted, and in the distance I saw something that set me thinking; it was a sweep of fir trees. Enlightenment came in a flash. "Yonder lie the Tow river," I said to an imaginary host with the pride of a Hannibal addressing the legions whom he had safely led across a mountain range and with this conviction I made a resolution, that I would now travel south only till I reached the Tow, which I was bound to do sooner or later if only I knew which was south.

Thereupon I set out for the distant fir trees, and reaching them in a couple of hours found myself in a good sized valley, running in a direction parallel to the one I had started from that morning, and evidently tributary to some larger valley at no great distance; it was this latter valley that I approached with a curious sense of trepidation, so much depended on it. The scenery, these bold crags and fir-clad cliffs, was that of the Tow river, yet being continually at fault had made me doubtful of myself, so that it was in a spirit of mingled apprehension and hope that I approached the valley mouth. As I turned the last shoulder I saw the gleam of water through the trees, and the roar of rapids broke on my ears, but even with this evidence, such was my morbid disbelief in my own good fortune that I had to invent the ridiculous fear that the river might be flowing in the wrong direction! Finally I emerged from the defile and pushed through the bushes.

There sparkled the Tow river, rippling through the tree clothed valley to plunge with a rattle and a roar over the rocks lower down; and never to Coptic pilgrim was the first sight of the Jordan more enchanting.

Gratitude at my deliverance from the Philistines was the thought uppermost in my mind, the ravages of hunger next; an overwhelming thirst I had been able to satisfy since leaving the ridge.

So far my position had been so embarrassing that I had had leisure to think neither of hunger nor of weariness, but now that I was on the right track both began to assert themselves. Yet strange to say I found it quite impossible to swallow the small remaining portion of bread, and it was not till I had mashed it up into fine paste with water that I was able to drink it down.

I calculated that it must now be near midday, and it was with the prospect of a good tea and sound sleep at the mission house in Chone that I presently set out eastwards down the river.

I was soon to learn the error of my presumption, however, for the narrow river here rolled between tremendously high wooded mountains which showed no immediate inclination to accommodate themselves to the more open valley and barer hills around Chone.

Tea gradually expanded into supper and supper dwindled into the realms of romance with the dropping sun, and still I walked on, apparently a long way yet from Chone.

The sun had set and the short twilight was fast waning when I presently found myself at the mouth of a valley which at once struck me as bearing the strongest resemblance in its general conformation to that in which Tow-chow was situated. In any case, it being impossible to reach Chone that night, it seemed worth while to hazard the chance of reaching Tow-chow direct, for there would be no great harm done were I mistaken.

But I was not mistaken, and had not proceeded far up this valley before I met a Chuanian who informed me that the city was indeed only a few miles distant.

Darkness had now fallen, but I continued for another hour in the hope of reaching the mission station that night; however progress became slower and slower for I was continually brought up short, ploughing through all sorts of liquid and semi-liquid obstructions, till at length, no sign of the city being visible, I gave it up and once more sat down for a night's rest.

For a time the new moon, hanging low over the ink-lined hills, shone brightly, but presently clouds sailed up and obscured the heavens, though the threatening rain held off. It was a raw night nevertheless and from time to time I dozed uneasily, cramped into cat-like positions for the sake of keeping out the wind and retaining some warmth. Never did night seem to drag along more slowly; with daylight as I continued to remind myself gleefully, I should be sitting down to a hot breakfast, but the goddess of dawn seemed to take an impish delight in torturing my patience by the protracted delay of her next appearance.

At last day broke and I made out the city barely two miles distant, nor was it long before I reached it. I was most kindly received by Mr. Simpson, and at six o'clock was enjoying a hearty breakfast and recounting my experiences on the plateau.

Three days later we left Tow-chow, returning by Chone and Min-chow as we had come, and thence striking the Chinese road to the south and Su-chuan.

8

The Sunny South

ACCUSTOMED AS we are in England to the gradual, almost casual change from one season to another, for example, from the cold of winter through a tiresome succession of intermediate types and temperatures, most of them vile, to the genial warmth of spring, a mutation, sudden and pronounced, comes as an agreeable surprise.

When we left Min-chou on 21st April it was emphatically winter. Leaden skies and bitter, gusty winds continually threatened snow, and bare hillsides suggested that nothing dare show itself yet.

Crossing the main watershed for the last time at no great altitude above Minchou, we began the long and tedious descent of the deep valleys in which the Pa-shui-ho, a tributary of the Kia-ling, has its origin; and at once the scene was transformed.

The mountain sides sparkled with patches of emerald-green wheat, the villages were smothered beneath masses of pink and white fruit blossom, relieved along the mill streams by the fresh yellow-green of the poplar trees, and the mountain roads were gay with roses, yellow poppies, and blue irises; in three days we had stepped from winter into the midst of spring.

That night it rained, gently at first, later in torrents, till we were compelled in self defence to get up and seek cosy corners where the rain was not coming through the roof quite so unconcernedly. It was the first rain we had heard for six months, and no music could have sounded sweeter in our ears.

Amongst these rather arid mountains of southern Kansu, we encountered some of the worst pieces of road that had yet fallen to our share, and for several days our lot was not a happy one. The valley in many places narrowed to a deep gorge through the limestone, with sheer cliffs dipping precipitously into the river. In order to negotiate these sections, the road had been carried along the face of the precipice in the form of a bracket, barely three feet wide, supported on wooden props, jammed diagonally into the rock crevices below, the bracket thus hanging directly over the racing water, at a height varying from ten to thirty feet. In other places, the road had been cut out of the solid rock, and under such circumstances frequently ascended the face of the cliff to as much as two hundred feet above the torrent. With the usual frugality of native engineers these roads had been built with just that expenditure of time and material which would suffice, and a mule carrying an ordinary native load could get through.

But there was no margin, and for our mules with their bulky loads, the road was frequently impassable.

Under such conditions, we were compelled to take the loads off and carry them past the awkward places, an occupation which, though tedious and causing much delay, was attended with little difficulty, except in a few particularly narrow places, where the road rose a hundred feet or more above the river.

The real difficulty was occasioned when just sufficient room remained for the animals to get through provided that they kept calm, and one severe lesson taught us that it was expedient always to unload them unless there was a wide margin.

We were on a bracket hanging thirty feet above the river, and four of the animals had successfully passed a difficult corner.

As the last mule started on the venture however, his load struck against a projection, and the wretched creature immediately got in a panic. He was already, of course, on the extreme edge of the bracket, and the mishap evidently brought it home to his muddy mind that he was inconveniently near the river, for he now tried to crowd up against the cliff, whether with the idea of pushing it aside, or crawling up it, or merely with a hazy notion of getting as far from the brink as possible, I know not.

The result was the same in any case, for his load preventing him from embracing the cliff as he would have liked, he slewed across the narrow track, still butting manfully, but ineffectually against the rock wall.

It was an anxious moment. Two muleteers in front caught hold of his head, and three of us behind laid on to his tail, and by dint of much pulling we straightened him out again, though the load was now badly jammed against the cliff.

Just as safety seemed assured, however, the mule again became restive, and the edge of the bracket, unaccustomed to such antics, gave way under him, letting down one of his hind feet, while the load, already much out of place from contact with the cliff, assumed a threatening angle, as though about to topple bodily out of the pack-saddle.

Nor was our position behind very secure, as with feet braced against the crumbling edge of the bracket, we clung desperately at considerable personal risk, to the peevish beast's tail, fully prepared, should he resolve to take the plunge, to let go and not follow; it would have implied a bath taken with immodest precipitation, and a rough and ready massage on the rocks of altogether too generous vehemence.

When at length the mule was safely fixed again, the muleteers performed the gymnastic feat of grovelling under his belly and, balanced on the very edge of the bracket, of lifting the load sufficiently for him to back out from beneath it, after which the rest was easy.

I cite this incident, though unattended by serious consequences, as one of the many diversions which lend point to life on the road, and as a warning to those who travel through the mountains of western China with loads of unusual bulk. In this way we covered stages without a mishap and reached Kai-chow, a neat little city in an iron district, situated on an alluvial tongue of land sloping out fanwise from the mountains and jutting into the river.

Three days later came disaster. The road here was comparatively broad and about forty feet above the river.

Suddenly there were loud cries from the muleteers, fifty yards in the rear, and I turned round in time to sight a few odd garments, limp and water-logged, hurtling through the rapids. One of the loads was in the river.

Mechanically slipping off our coats, we climbed down the cliff and scrambled with all haste to the scene of the accident where a half sinking mass of shattered pack-rack, stove-in boxes, and tangled ropes, edied slowly round and round, a few feet from the shore, approaching, perilously near to the rapids as its gyrations gradually increased in circumference.

Had the load floated out of the cove, to which it was at present confined, nothing could have saved it from being dashed to pieces in a few minutes, but by the aid of a long pole which was happily forthcoming, we secured it before this crowning misfortune occurred, and hauling the remnants up the cliff, took stock of the damage.

It was bad enough, and while we covered the sunny side of the rocks with books and specimens laid out to dry, the boxes and pack-rack were temporarily repaired; so that two hours later we were able to continue our journey.

Our old friend the mutinous cliff climb mule was responsible for the accident.

Contrary to his principles, he was trudging along bravely on the edge of the path, when it suddenly gave way under him, and his hind quarters came down with a bump, tipping the load out of the saddle. So lightened, he recovered himself with an effort, but the load had crashed down the rocks and rolled into the river.

We were now compelled to remain idle for two days, while the damaged specimens were thoroughly dried; many of my most cherished photographs had been irreparably ruined, but except for that and the loss of a few personal effects, there was no great harm done.

Continuing down the valley, we reached Pi-kow, a fen-hsien city at the head of navigation on the Pa-shui-ho already referred to. As in most places where there is a boating or mining population, we found the people extremely curious and inclined to be rowdy, though not hostile, while the inns were atrocious even for Kansu.

Next day we left the river, and, continuing south, climbed a couple of thousand feet up into the mountains again, stopping to do our last work in Kansu at a spot twenty miles from the border.

There was no village, only a few inns at intervals down the valley, and we were fortunate enough to obtain an outhouse to ourselves in a quiet and isolated hostelry. Before we had been three days in the place, however, an extraordinary incident occurred, when early one morning the old innkeeper's son arrived from Pi- kow, twenty miles back, in a great state of perturbation.

In the course of conversation later in the day, the reason for this desertion of business in order to visit his parents, came out.

Some muleteers, it appeared, who had passed the inn and gone on to Pi-kow on the previous day, had reported there a wild fabrication, to the effect that the foreigners who were travelling that road, had beaten the innkeeper, broken the back of his horse and generally played havoc with the inn. Naturally when this story came to the young man's ears, he at once left his business and hurried into the mountains, very ill at ease, to see how his father was, and what he could do to mend matters; only to find, to his astonishment, perfect peace reigning.

A more villainious travesty of the truth could hardly have been devised. "Why," said his mother," they give less trouble than the ordinary guests, and there has not been a word of complaint on either side"; which was quite true, for we were particularly friendly with the inn people, simple and kind folk.

When we left, a few days later, the innkeeper insisted on our accepting a small present of flour, and made us promise that if we were ever in that part of Kansu again, we would once more honour his humble roof.

The young man, much relieved to find his fears groundless, now returned to to Pi-kow in a more comfortable frame of mind, let us hope, to spread abroad a very different story to that which had brought him hot haste to his ruined home.

We heard a good deal of gossip from time to time about the ill-treatment of natives by foreigners, and unfortunately we know that some of the incidents referred to were only too true.

Men have openly boasted that they have travelled half across the country without disbursing a single cash, and others have earned an ugly reputation for emphasizing their orders by the display of, or the theatrical suggestion of, physical violence.

In dealing with Chinese as in dealing with any other uneducated people, especially Asiatics, it is sometimes necessary to employ force, if you mean to have your own way; but there are ways and means and degrees of applying it, differing in men and beasts.

Certain Americans, Germans, Frenchmen, even Britons on occasion, have left an indelible and despicable impression amongst the natives.

One person, the author of several well advertised if little read books on China, had created an atmosphere — not a very bracing one either, in almost every big city we stopped at: there was not a white man of any nationality, of the many we met who had come in contact with him, but spoke of him with contempt.

Moreover we had every reason to believe in many of these stories, since we ourselves had the misfortune to come into daily contact with a creature of a peculiarly contemptible type, who, unable to control either his temper or impatience, displayed far more boorish stupidity than the ignorant, kindly peasants amongst whom we travelled. He never used force, such people never do, but contented himself with a sulky silence or, flying to the other extreme, with an impudent air of brag and bounce, and overbearing truculence which amazed us.

I do not hesitate to say that, had it not been for the tact and knowledge of Dr. Smith, who sufficiently counteracted this evil influence amongst the natives, we should have found ourselves in a serious situation on more than one occasion, apart from the fact that, without native help, the expedition would have proved zoologically almost a fiasco.

This person has made substantial additions to his country's national debt in China, if not to the latter's exchequer.

The pity of it is that the open-handed liberality of the missionaries should be so disgracefully abused by these imps. Still, it is necessary to be on one's guard in accepting vernacular reports, though it is unlikely that deliberate lies are often bruited about. "There are no waves without wind," to quote a familiar Chinese proverb, and while a liberal discount for the Asiatic's love of exaggeration, such stories as a rule have some foundation in fact.

On 12th May, we finally set out for Cheng-tu, crossed the pass into Su-chuan guarded by an old wall, the open gate of which had long since ceased to swing on its hinges, and descended into the rich vales of the south.

Crossing another high pass on the following day, we obtained a fine view of the snow-clad ranges around Sung-pau, far away in the west, and descended into the basin of the Min river, not far from Lo-gan-fu.

We had not been in this lovely province three days, however, when at Ching-chuan, a fen-hsien city, the ordinary routine of inn hospitality was again roughly jarred.

This incident may be regarded as the inevitable sequel to the communistic system in vogue amongst Chinese inn-keepers, though such a thing had never occurred before.

Into these literally public houses, any idler may wander out of sheer curiosity, saunter round the premises, inspect the guests and their property, at leisure, chat with the inn-keeper or his servants, kick the dog, and wander out again without having spent a cash; and when foreigners arrive, they make full use of the privilege, privacy being a luxury we rarely enjoyed.

Our host on this occasion was a Mohammedan, and we found ourselves not very welcome guests. With the usual smug air of self-satisfaction so frequently adopted by these men, he informed us that we were not wanted, and that the inn was not for guests, nor was he dependent upon it for a living.

This lack of hospitality made no difference to us of course. The man had elected to throw open an inn, and we elected to stay there, whether he had opened it merely for fun, or for anything else. And before we had been there an hour the head muleteer had his bundle of clothes stolen.

No sooner was the discovery made than the innkeeper was

informed of the fact, and requested to find the thief, but with irritating procrastination he and his servants whiled away an hour, glibly protesting their complete ignorance of the outrage and loudly denying all responsibility.

There were no bad characters round his inn, he said, and he could not know everybody who came in from outside. To which the muleteer replied that he obviously could not know the stray characters who came into the inn, since he was a stranger there, and that if the inn-keeper allowed anyone to stroll into his inn and into rooms occupied by his guests, then he was responsible for the safety of their property — a just enough plea.

The man, however, persisted in denying his liability, and carried his bluff just as far as it would go for, Dr. Smith now appearing on the scene, the matter was put plainly enough. He must either find the stolen goods, or — we must appeal to the yamen; and should the latter refuse to interfere — an unlikely contingency, then we must obtain redress at the capital later.

The effect of the word yamen was instantaneous, and the inn-keeper, finally abandoning his intolerable air of aloofness, cringed limply. He begged that such extreme measures would not be resorted to, and promised to take what steps he could to recover the stolen articles; useless talking also ceased, for the star orator had collapsed like a pricked bladder.

Next morning, however, nothing had been done, and our cards went to the yamen, the official at once sending round his assistant to enquire into the circumstances of the case on our behalf, while the head of the local gentry was summoned to represent the inn-keeper as it were, and act as middleman, this being the usual course of procedure in such disputes.

There was no difficulty about the matter. The yamen official at once ordered the inn-keeper to produce the articles or to pay up, and he had to do so. Moreover the mediator's suggestion that we should be lenient and let him off with half was ignored, the inn-keeper's boast that he was not dependent upon his inn now recoiling upon himself; if he could afford to open an inn for fun he could afford to pay the claim in full.

No better combination of circumstances for commissions on every hand could be devised. Mark what happens. The yamen indemnifies the muleteer, probably because the inn-keeper has not sufficient silver in hand.

It recoups itself at leisure from the latter, adding a small percentage on its own account.

Finally the yamen and the inn-keeper between them hunt down the thief, and compel him to disgorge the booty, and to pay the latter out of all proportion to his frustrated gains under pain of a lingering imprisonment.

We did not, of course, stay to see all this accomplished, but in the ordinary course of Chinese justice it assuredly will come to pass, and the thief be caught.

Every district has its own head of the thieves, who must receive his own share of each petty theft, and the subordinate responsible for all this trouble would doubtless be apprehended through him — for a consideration. On the other hand, should he attempt to carry the thing through entirely on his own account, he lays himself open to the wrath of his chief, who would have no scruples about bleeding him white and then handing him over to the yamen, as an example to bumptious underlings! Had the muleteer not been an honest man, he would have added fifty per cent to his loss; as it was he stated exactly what each article had cost and deducted a certain amount in consideration of the fact that some of the clothes had been worn a few times.

Not long afterwards we were out of the mountains, emerging through some splendid limestone gorges, into the foot-hills of the red basin, a beautiful country of undulating cultivated land, the brilliant green of the rice fields blending with the red hill tops to form a wonderfully coloured landscape.

Through the cup-like hollows which dimpled the country in every direction, numerous shining streams wound their way in and out like silver threads, while here and there a slender pagoda rose above the tree tops and pricked the blue sky.

In order to irrigate the terraced hillsides from these streams, an ingenious arrangement was resorted to.

Immense framework wheels, built entirely of bamboo except for their solid axles, were set slowly in motion by the stream flowing against a series of paddles, as in an ordinary undershot mill-wheel, and between each pair of paddles was fixed a hollow bamboo tube, closed at one end, making an angle of 45° to a tangent through the point of attachment. This diagonal setting of the tubes against the circumference caused those at the top and bottom of the wheel to be tilted slightly downwards and upwards respectively, while in intermediate places they approached the upright and inverted position.

Consequently a tube carried the stream as the wheel revolved, scooped up water and retained it till it reached the top, where, tilting over gradually, it emptied itself into a trough, and descended to be refilled, a continuous flow of water into the trough being thus maintained by the upcoming tubes as long as the wheel revolved. These irrigation wheels, often as much as thirty feet high, usually stood in rows, eight or ten together being no uncommon sight, and the whining and screeching of the slowly revolving monsters was extraordinary.

At the Tsung-pa, a large market-town where the Church Missionary Society have an outstation, we learnt with deep regret of the death of our Sovereign, only eleven days after the sad event. The news had been telegraphed from Shanghai to Chengtu, and had just come up by post.

THE SUNNY SOUTH

A very long stage on the following day brought us to Mienchow, on the verge of the great Chengtu plain. As we approached the city in the evening we were surprised to see a crowd of natives, about twenty-five a-side, playing football on a sort of grassy pebble beach near the river, while a foreign gentleman dispensed justice with a whistle.

Interest in the breathless encounter now suddenly flagged, and wheeling round, focussed itself full upon the dishevelled looking foreigners tramping citywards, who were presently greeted by Mr. Taylor, the dispensor of justice. We now entered the city in triumph with our host, while the remainder of the football teams — all those who had not bitten the dust of the pebble beach, formed a guard of honour in the rear.

First to the school, we had already seen the boys at play, and we were now to see where they worked. Here we found clean, neatly dressed little scholars, and schoolrooms which could vie with any in Shanghai for size, comfort and equipment.

Pride of place is given to the Chinese Classics, but English, history, and geography are also taught, the two latter in the Chinese language of course, though in the case of arithmetic the ordinary Arabic cyphers are employed.

After that we obtained a glimpse of the church, a quaint building in the Chinese style, which gave it a somewhat serio comic air of pristine sanctity beyond its years, and finally were ushered into the foreign compound.

It was a jolly evening, one of the jolliest we remember, for our new friends gave us a royal reception. Mr. Taylor turned out to be an old Cambridge man, only a couple of years senior to me, and delving into the past, buried but not forgotten, we resurrected many a delightful episode and cherished name, associated for ever with the gray colleges by the Cam.

Another gentleman, Mr. Watt, a keen botanist, had been

associated with some of my old friends and teachers, and we talked of books and men, and of the wonderful flowers of China.

A third gentleman, by name Mr. Spreckley, told us of the West African coast, where he had spent some years, and in these delightful circumstances it may be imagined how the evening, all too fleeting, passed; though only the thought of an early start next day, at a late hour induced us to take leave and seek our inn, whether the mules had preceded us.

Another stage, and we were down on the dead level plain, the road now deeply ribbed, as many as eight or ten parallel grooves, worn by the countless wheelbarrows which for ages have plied to and fro across the plain, cutting up the flagstones for miles.

One of the most remarkable features of this plain is the number of rapidly flowing rivers which traverse it at frequent intervals, spanned by arched bridges of red sandstone, many of them with finely carved parapets ornamented with quaint gargoyles.

These rivers, usually from twenty to thirty yards across, are, as a matter of fact, artificial canals, which diverge from the Minho at Kuan-hsien, some distance to the north of Chengtu, traverse the plain in a number of parallel arcs, and converge again upon the river south of the capital.

Undertaken at the instance of one of the emperors more than two thousand years ago, this tremendous scheme of irrigation converted the previously parched Chengtu plain into one of the most fertile and densely populated regions in the world, teeming with prosperous cities and villages, and cultivated to the last acre under every variety of crop.

On our march of 22nd May, villages became more frequent, gradually merged into one long hive swarming with human beings, and culminated beneath the walls of the capital of Szechwan.

So smothered beneath its canopy of trees and houses is the

plain, that the great gate is not visible above the roofs of the interminable street till one is within half a mile of it, already sucked into the vortex of the whirl of coolies and wheelbarrows which gurgles with ever increasing velocity towards the narrow entrance, and, rushing through, spreads slowly out into the vast city; a very different sight to that which greets the traveller as he approaches Hsian-fu, visible for a distance of several miles, and enters the huge gate choked with its roaring mule traffic, to hear through the clouds of dust the grinding and rumbling of wheels on cobbles, the crack of the long whips, and yelling of frenzied muleteers.

9

Cheng-Tu

It is a wonderful city, this Cheng-tu. Situated on the Min river, in the heart of a great plain, 1700 feet above sea level, accessible from the coast 2000 miles distant by boat, it is the metropolis of the west.

Cheng-tu does not appear to have ever played a leading role in history, and the antiquarian searching for historic monuments is likely to be disappointed.

Thw rebel Chang hsien-tsung, however, who upset the Ming dynasty at the end of the 17th century, seems to have earned a very evil reputation in the province, and there is said to be still extant, though now behind brick walls, a pillar on which is engraved his tirade against mankind in general ending up with the bare words: "Kill! Kill! Kill!" which advice, before offering to the public, he seems to have put into practice very effectually himself.

Originally quite a harmless person he presently fell on evil times and, his cup of bitterness full to overflowing, he was one day unlucky enough, being ignorant of the properties of stinging nettles, to sit down on a bed of them. It was the straw that broke the camel's back. Impelled to his feet by the reception accorded him he yelled: Why, even the weeds of this cursed country are against me! Whereupon, realising that be had even incurred the

CHENG-TU

displeasure of the despised weeds, he hardened his heart and wreaked vengeance on all and sundry, seriously decimating the population of Szechwan by his enmity towards the human race.

Well known to Europeans, being scarcely off the beaten road in the interior, much has doubtless been written about the capital of Szechwan; nevertheless, at a time when the country is endeavouring, with renewed energy, to cast off the cloak of conservatism and appear before the world in a new garment, it will be of interest to again bring it into notice.

Of all the western provinces, Szechwan is pre-eminently the most progressive, as it is also the richest, and the capital worthily sets the example. No sooner is he inside the gates, than the newcomer feels instinctively that here at least is a city which reflects the future of China.

Populous as it is, there is not here the appalling crush of such a city as Canton, for the main streets are of ample width; neither choking dust nor rumbling carts as in Peking or Hsian, for the streets are stone paved throughout, and vehicular traffic is unknown in the south; neither are there filthy thoroughfares ankle deep in black mud and offal, as in the crowded parts of Nanking; instead, the streets are kept surprisingly clean and wholesome. Wheelbarrows there are, restricted, however, to certain streets where a gutter, running down the centre, is provided for them. A few dilapidated ricshas amble slowly along, and a man on horseback clears the street with a jingle of bells as he heralds the approach of an official borne aloft in his chair by six or eight hurrying bearers. But that is all, and under such conditions it is a pleasure not a nightmare to be out on the streets. The critic may complain, not altogether justly, that the policemen are mere wooden images dozing at their posts all day long and never venturing beyond the street corner; but where there is no traffic to keep them alert, one cannot expect to find the guardians of the law and order much in evidence, and a street row is the rarest of sights. Moreover, the army of beggars who infest every road outside the city are not allowed to prosecute their calling within the walls of this Celestial Utopia, but are sent to work in a penitentiary, which, however, is by no means a prison, unless enforced labour from all able-bodied mea found begging may be regarded as a restraint on the freedom of the person.

Splendid shops add colour to the sunlit streets, shaded here and there with bamboo matting stretched from house to house, or by wistaria trees roofing it over with leafy arch. Rows of embroidery shops, men hard at work carving wood or polishing jade, cloth weavers with hand looms, fur merchants displaying leopard, wolf and otter skins, silk merchants, and many others attract attention till we come to the arcade.

The arcade is rather out of place. Briefly, it is a facsimile of Foochow road, Shanghai, its high balconied two story shops displaying every variety of cheap foreign goods from a bottle of spurious cognac to a hair-brush with a looking-glass in the back. Scented soap, oil lamps, clocks, coffee-pots and a host of similar Japanese manufactures find a ready sale amongst the wealthy Chinese here, who love to display their western culture.

At night; the arcade is brilliantly illuminated by means of incandescent and arc lamps, aa3 tho dazzling appearance of polished metal, glass, and tinsel under this pitiless glare is too much for the cupidity of the young bloods, who frequent the arcade after dusk; fascinated by the scintillating display, they now flutter helplessly from shop to shop, like gaudy moths round an arc lamp, and promote a roaring trade. Chengtu is not, of course, a treaty-port, nor is it ever likely to be one, so that it seems at first rather a contradiction to find a British Consul ensconced here; but in view of the fact that the foreign population connected with the missions, colleges and Imperial

Post Office is over a hundred, of whom the great majority are British subjects, it is not unreasonable that His Britannic Majesty should be adequately represented. However, we may surmise that an equally straight-forward but far more subtle policy than that of affording protection to British subjects, underlay the project at its inception. A precedent for such action it afforded by the British Consul at Yunnan-fu, but in consideration of the fact that the frontier of Yunnan marches for seven hundred miles with that of British Burma, coupled with the presence of the French railway from Hanoi, it is not surprising that we should insist on safeguarding our interests there by establishing a consulate in the capital.

In 1901 Sir Alexander Hosie quietly left Chung-king and went up to Chengtu, where he settled down without any unnecessary fuss. His first step was to send in his card to the Viceroy, who hearing what was in the wind, returned the compliment, but pointedly sent his card to Chungking, a polite hint to tho Consul where he ought to be. This, however, had no effect. Sir A. Hosie had come to stay, and in spite of a campaign of unobtrusive hostility, refused to budge, till at last his persistence triumphed, and official recognition was accorded him. Mr. Wilkinson, the present Consul-General, however, informed me that when the Viceroy wishes to be sarcastically distant, as he does when offended in any matter, such as the presence of British gunboats at Kiating-fu, he still addresses him, after eight years practice, as Consul-General, Chung-king. Whatever other nations may have thought of the matter as a diplomatic victory reflecting on their own lack of initiative, at least they were not going to allow any scruples about China's welfare to stand in the way of their profiting by Great Britain's move. Doubtless it seemed better to acquiesce and fall into line, than, by playing the part of disinterested champion of China's liberty — a role which had already been played on another stage with conspicuous lack of success — cause trouble.

Hence French and German consulates are now established at Chengtu, with the prospect of joining in the choras at least, but it may be questioned whether they are present for any other purpose than that of fulfilling, like the chorus girl, always delightful but not indispensable, the humble duty of watching. The position of German Consul, in particular, seems almost as great a sinecure as does that of Cuban Consul in Shanghai. The British Consulate is a transformed native compound situate in a quiet by-way near the centre of the city. Mr. Wilkinson, a charming companion with a weakness for "bridge," took great interest in our journey, and made minute inquiries into the state of the crops, the cultivation of opium, the attitude of the people, and other pregnant questions, fragments which, fitted together with a host of similar fragments from all sources, go to make up the Chinese puzzle complete sent in to the foreign office. The Consul, however, lamented humorously over his situation. "Here am I living in this hole" he said," while my missionaries live in palaces."

Yet personally I was rather struck by the comfort and elegance of the Consulate; it was not indeed in this respect that it failed in comparison with many of the mission stations, but in its immediate surroundings. Situated in a street so narrow that, on the occasion of the King's death, it had been blocked from end to end by the retinues of the seventy officials who had come to offer their condolence to the representative of the British Empire, it is closely invested on all sides by small native houses, which are never conducive to a savoury atmosphere, while the congestion naturally precludes the idea of lawns.

On the day of the late King's funeral, this, the most remote of all British Consulates, was the scene of an impressive memorial

CHENG-TU

service in the presence of the entire foreign population; impressive, perhaps, beyond the dreams of more favourably situated communities, for in such distant places where arrangements for special functions have to be made hurriedly and under heavy liabilities, in the matter of symbolical representation, the deep note of human emotion, unfettered by the pomp and glitter of ceremony, is more free to express itself loyally, naturally and simply.

And the missionaries of Chengtu, what are we to say of them?

There are four missions at work here, but the only one to which reference need be made is the Canadian Methodist, a standing example of what a mission should be. A distinguished missionary and scholar has said: "Show the Chinese that you are a little better than them in everything, that your houses, your dress, your education, are superior to theirs, and they will conclude that your religion must be better too."

It is no doubt this policy of "going one better" that underlies the undoubted success of the Canadian Mission in Chengtu. Here they do things in style, from the splendid residential quarter, with its wide sweeps of well trimmed lawns, on the outskirts of the city, to the university, the printing press, and the magnificent three-storied hospital, now in course of construction,

The press is well worth a visit. Undertaking all printing for western China, it prints pamphlets in Tibetan and Miao-tsi as well as in English and Chinese. Between sixty and seventy men and boys are employed in the type setting, printing, binding, and other departments, turning out 6,000 booklets a day, a supply which hardly keeps pace with the demand, so that the mission is already thinking of establishing a second press in Chungking. The university scheme is the result of a combination of several missions, each contributing a certain sum for educational purposes.

At present the teaching is being carried on in temporary premises, but the site for the future buildings, just outside the city, has been obtained, and the work will shortly be put in hand.

As yet, the teaching of science is in its infancy in China, and the difficulty of translating technical language into the vernacular, with sufficient terseness, is considerable.

Useful elementary works on botany, zoology, chemistry and other subjects have, however, already been translated both by European and Chinese scholars, and not many years will have elapsed before the students will be able to acquire a proficient training in science without going abroad for it.

But it is the modern hospital, now nearing completion, which makes the lay mind gasp—an immense building, heir of all the ages in knowledge and equipment for meeting human bodily suffering.

Its chief features may be briefly summed up; accommodation for 135 beds with private suites of rooms and verandas for wealthy patients, private quarters for two trained European nurses, operating theatres, x-ray room, pathological and anatomical research laboratories, chemical laboratory, demonstrating rooms—in short, a complete self-contained hospital and medical school.

And then we are told that it is the first of a series of six or eight hospitals for western Szechwan, the money to carry out a ten years' building programme being already subscribed!

The Canadian Methodist Mission, in fact, lays down hospitals just as easily as the British Government lays down Dreadnoughts.

Such facts as these bring home to one more forcibly that the missionary is not merely a voice crying in the wilderness. On the contrary the missionary is first of all a reformer who is aiming, through the fundamental medium of religion, at bettering the whole life of the nation. A healthy religion is the basis of good government and sound commerce, and Young China is being prepared in this to-day.

Above all, the Canadian contingent, and I met many of them, both in the capital and on Omi-san, are intensely human.

The cynic who believes that the missionary is a sort of star— Sinus I suppose, for is there not, according to this authority, something of the Cerberus about him?—something aloof and singular, but also something cold and critical, looking with unblinking yet disdainful eye on a wicked world, something to admire in a detached sort of manner, but also something to avoid, as being beyond the unspanned gulf the cynic who paints the missionary of the interior in these colours would do well to visit Chengtu.

I did not find anybody cold, or critical, or aloof, and the Canadian girls were very nice indeed to me; but no one mistook me for a saint.

Comparisons are odious, and I do not for one moment intend to institute a comparison between the Canadian Methodist and other missions, all of which are actuated by a common impulse— the welfare of China. Of course this mission is particularly wealthy, and Chengtu is a particularly well situated centre. But many a missionary in the interior who now lives in a Chinese compound would, and ought to, live in an European house—if be could. But he can't, and for a similar reason he is not in a position to build hospitals or printing presses. And what is the effect of all this teaching? What place is Christianity taking in the revival of the nation?

Probably the Chinaman, all-practical as he is, does see the benefits to be derived from an active form of Christianity, and will gradually come to adopt it as a working hypothesis— become in fact Christian by nature while remaining heathen by choice.

Two things militate against the success of this attempted evangelization of China. In the first place, the Chinese are being westernized in other matters as rapidly as in religious matters, and in the delight of novelty and the pursuit of pleasure, religion is apt to be swamped. In the second place, this enterprise, starting from the general, which is indefinitely great, hopes to reach the particular, which is definitely small. In other words it is the masses who are being taught the doctrine, the classes who are not, and cannot, be, touched.

If only a small proportion of the officials were Christians, China would belong to Christendom in a year. But I never yet heard of an official who professed Christianity, and without this, failure seems foredoomed; for the new religion, as a religion, appeals to the ignorant and superstitious, not to the wealthy and influential.

The grafting of a new religion on an old people has been hailed by many as likely to lead to as complete disaster as putting new wine into old bottles, for history teems with examples of the gradual disintegration of state or empire, as it fell away from the religions ideals which had given it birth, and from which it had sucked up life to grow, strength to thrive, and to conquer.

Venice and Spain, names for all time, are now but the ashes of Empires which have fertilized the soil for those who came after.

Just as soon as religion is dissociated from life, and becomes something apart, a routine, a thing to examine critically from afar, so soon is man divorced from himself, and a nation is visited with the sins of its sons. But China has striven for centuries with the caricature of a once noble religion, which was never national, popular, and always thwarted by a creed which, though not a religion, is certainly a national product, and deeply appealing.

Herein lies the hope of her accepting the doctrines of Christianity, for it is an acknowledged fact that a people must adopt some form of worship, whether it is the nature-worship of primitive man, the graven images of polytheism, or the monotheistic religion of more advanced civilization.

Brave Christianity they will doubtless accept, at least the ethics of social intercourse between man and man, as set forth in scripture; for it is the tangible outcome of abstract principles, which appeals to Chinese common sense; and with this to weld them together, they will assume their true place in the world. After all, the Chinese may be corrupt, but they are not luxurious; cruel, but they are not barbarous; irreligious, but they are not immoral.

Reform is at present sporadic, growing from well established centres of infection, but the pabulum on which it is being cultivated is widely spread, and the radius of action increases rapidly. Individual waves may roll forward only to retreat again, but the tide is coming on.

On the other hand it must not be assumed that the impetus for reform is derived entirely from outside sources; the seeds of progress are being sown from high quarters in Szechwan.

Amongst the more important government institutions in the capital are the arsenal, an up-to-date factory in a somewhat chaotic condition owing to the lack of shilled workmen who are completely conversant with their tools; the mint, which, by issuing rupees and dollars, makes the local currency far more amenable to deal with, if rather more involved beyond a limited radius; and several educational establishments, in particular the Railway School and the University. The former, attended by some two hundred students, many of whom have previously studied abroad and are proficient in the English language, is staffed chiefly by Chinese, though there are two or three foreigners teaching higher mathematics. and engineering; from time to time drafts of students are ordered to proceed to Peking, where they undergo advanced training in railway work.

The university also employs several foreign teachers in addition to a large Chinese staff. The students number over two hundred, but the majority of them are hardly acquainted with English, so that the foreign teachers are compelled to instruct them through the medium of interpreters — a very unsatisfactory state of affairs. We must not blind ourselves whither the present movement is leading. It cannot be many years before China will herself be in a position to undertake the education of her people along rational lines, and no ambition could be more natural or more worthy.

What we, as her friends, should urge her against, is any attempt to embark upon such a mission before she is ready. There has been a recent tendency to replace capable foreign teachers, in her schools and colleges, by men who have a mere veneer, a Japanned film of superficial knowledge, and the results are deplorable.

It can only mean a postponement of emancipation from foreign supervision, since a poor teacher invariably trains still poorer disciples; the movement defeats its own object, and becomes a retrograde one. The real test of a great teacher is, that his brightest pupils learn to rise even higher than himself.

In this respect, China has behaved like an impulsive and precocious child, spoiling to leave the nursery before her time. It is inevitable that she will be ready to leave soon, but to do so prematurely is to nullify all that has gone before.

Finally the cavalry barracks and magnificent parade ground call for comment, the Szechwan army being one must infer (for the flower of it is now an active service), something more than no agglomeration of men with rifles. There was a band practice every evening on the parade ground, and though method did not enter conspicuously into the nightly programme, strains of

CHENG-TU

"Lead, kindly light" and other familiar hymns being sandwiched rather whimsically between selections from Mendolsohn's Songs without Words, and snatches from the latest opperetta, the music was quite successful. Tradition dies hard. As an example of the collision now brought about between new and old in these changing times, mention may be made of the funeral of the ti-'tio, the highest military official in the city, which took place while we were there. Nothing was omitted which proclaimed that it was a Chinese funeral, but on the other hand, much was included which suggested, in a crude way, that it was a military funeral in the twentieth century; and the clash of past and present made the pageant a bizarre one at best.

Passing over the emblematical part of the procession, which never seems to vary, we come to the immense coffin, supported on a centre pole made in the likeness of a dragon and borne on the shoulders of twenty-eight men. Clustered round it are the chief mourners, thirty or forty in number, dressed from head to foot in white, the leading gentleman bowed almost double as though with grief, and supported in this singularly uncomfortable and not very dignified position by a man on either side. The entire cortege is roped in by a string of men marching on either side and holding up a long white sash, which forms a sort of rail round the coffin and its attendant mutes.

Somehow the unreality of it all strikes one as farcical; everyone is so obviously insincere, so preoccupied with quite other matters, that it is scarcely flippant to add that the mourners looked more like a contingent of dissolute pastry-cooks than anything else.

Next comes the brass band playing bank-holiday airs with triumphant blare of trumpets and roll of drums, but the attempts of the soldiers behind to carry themselves with erect military bearing and to keep in step, would have moved a drill-sergeant to tears. Some were as stiff as ram-rods, others as limp as chewed string, and the combined effect was droll in the extreme.

Lastly, bringing up the rear comes a squad of little boys from one of the government schools, innocent little cherubs in ill-fitting khaki suits, trousers too long and coats too short and Brodrick caps. Obviously they don't know what they are there for, and are rather disconcerted by the crowds lining the streets; but determined to put a bold face on the matter, they hold each other's hands affectionately and shuffle merrily along, more like a troop of children on a fresh-air-fund spree than actors in the drama of a big military funeral.

So we leave Chengtu, the coming city of the west, not without a hope registered that the oft discussed, and already initiated railway, will one day bring it within easy reach of I-chang, and the great highway of China.

10

The Tibet Road

As early as the end of May the Chengtu plain lay under a burning sun, and we now hastened through this richly cultivated hothouse towards the dim mountains. Across rivers, now mere trickles of water, presently to be swollen by floods of rain from the hills, past guardian pagodas glistening white on many a bluff overlooking the city they protected, under scores of skilfully carved and painted p'ai-low, these triumphal arches spanning the highway every few hundred yards in the neighbourhood of a city or big market town, the dusty road soon led us back into the shade of the tree clad foot-hills.

Though it is, of course, pleasant to note what a number of virtuous widows, philanthropic officials, and other estimable persons the countryside has produced, as witnessed by these memorials erected to them, the evidence is to some extent nugatory, since it is whispered that the official himself is in many cases the sole judge of what constitutes a brilliant tenure of office, and has at his own expense generously decorated the landscape with a monument extolling his virtues; nor does the inscription as a rule err on the side of under-estimating either his ability or the services rendered to an appreciative public.

Five days' travel brought us to Ya-chow-fu under the shadow of the mountains, at the head of navigation on the Ya-ho, a tributary of the Min river, which it enters at Kiating-fu, and on the following day we plunged thankfully into the lower mountain valleys.

A day out from Ya-chow, a Japanese traveller arrived at the inn, late at night, from the west. He had been looking for a lost friend as he informed our cook, with disingenuous frankness, and to us confided the further information, that having been forbidden by the authorities to go from Batang into Yunnan direct, he was now returning to Chung-king, in order to follow the orthodox route.

He spoke English moderately badly, and sufficiently Chinese for his purpose, since he was quite alone. But it was his appearance that chiefly excited our curiosity, for his Chinese dress and long hair hanging loosely over his shoulders plainly told that he had quite recently been masquerading as a Chinaman, his only visible impedimenta being a blanket, carried like a horse-collar over his shoulder, military fashion. That he was in reality a spy on secret service I hardly doubted, a suspicion confirmed later when we learnt that he had never reached Batang at all, but had been politely escorted out of the Mantze country by the authorities. Curiously enough, when in Shensi and Kansu we had followed for several months in the wake of a Japanese traveller who had previously been selling patent medicines in that part of the country.

We heard of him on every hand in many a city and distant village, for he had evidently made a mark during the course of his travels, and it may be surmised that he elicited all the information he required from the simpletons who gaped at his quack drugs.

The truth is, Japanese spies have explored western China very thoroughly during the last few years and it is probable she possesses more first hand information about the country she

THE TIBET ROAD

hopes one day to control than any other Power.

A high barrier range which the clouds are evidently unable to navigate safely, since they cling desperately to the east slope, separates the village of Hwang-ni, on the east, from Ching-chi, the last hsien city on the Tatsienlu road, to the west.

Consequently while Hwang-ni revels in the midst of semi-tropical vegetation the hsien is withering on a sand-bank, which has the effect of putting the place to sleep.

The people rubbed their eyes and yawned like so many Rip Van Winkles when we disturbed them by coming through, but they failed to remark on any startling improvements that might have taken place while they had slept; nor did we notice any. We tried to obtain one or two simple articles of diet here, but the people only stared at us. "We haven't got that," they said wearily, adding in an apologetic tone before resuming their slumbers," this is Ching-chi"! which of course disposed of the whole matter at once.

It is a curiously situated city. Seen from the summit of the pass to the east it appears to be on a considerable plain in the valley below, protected by one wall only, built across the upper end of the valley.

Though the idea of a city with only one wall is rather incongruous, still one is hardly prepared, when viewing the city from the ridge at the lower end of the valley, to see how completely one has been misled by perspective.

The apparent plain on which the city stands is in reality a tongue of land projecting at a steep angle from the mountains above, and bounded on three sides by an almost sheer bluff two hundred feet high, formed by the excavations of two converging streams.

These streams, by cutting deeply through the soft sandstone and coalescing lower down the valley, have chiselled out this wedge and truncated its apex at their junction, and though the bluff so formed has been walled up on the outside for a height of ten or twelve feet from below, the top of the wall, being almost flush with the surface inside, is scarcely prominent from any distance, so that the city appears to have only the one barrier wall. Ching-chi-hsien may remind the Devonshire man of Clovelly if he is not hypercritical, for the main street goes down the steeply shelving hillside in a series of stone flagged steps. But it would need a company promoter to push the resemblance further. In Devonshire we say that Clovelly was the first place God ever made, and that He has been making it prettier ever since; but, if so, Ching-chi was surely one of the last, made in rather a hurry with a shortage of material, all other sites being already occupied.

Crossing a second high watershed at 10,000 feet into the basin of the T'ung river, we reached Wha-lin-ping, a small village near the head of the valley at an altitude of 8,000 feet amidst thickly wooded mountains, and finding it a quiet spot, settled down for a few days' work.

Wha-lin-ping presented the interesting spectacle of a village in decay, for, though of considerable size, at least half the houses stood empty, and business was so slack that nobody had the heart to open a shop, though in bursts of enthusiasm they had what they called market-days. Meanwhile babies who were not old enough to know better carried on a brisk trade hawking delicacies amongst the strings of coolies who passed along this road.

The mountain side behind was covered with thousands of graves, which it would certainly have taken centuries to fill at the present rate of increase of the population, though a man did die of sheer fatigue while we were there. The day previous to the funeral he lay in state, while his friends went in one by one and kotowed to the dead man, before dropping in on his relatives next door for a drink of wine — free. Then they came out yelling with laughter, all sadness banished by the cup that cheers, kotowed again, and returned once more to condole garrulously with the bereaved relatives, over another cup of wine; and through out the mock- solemn function they took turns to parade up and down the street in front of the house, banging drums and cymbals with brazen monotony, while the women folk inside kept up a continuous noisy chorus of unrestrained rending sobs. It was a sorry exhibition.

The gross luxury of dying, in China, though apparently one of the most deeply rooted characteristics of the nation, rich and poor alike, is a matter in need of urgent reform. No man can die without crippling the finances of his family, and if they die in squads, it spells ruin for someone.

One of our own servants was a case in point. His father, a man of position and some property, was a major in the army, but on his death at a somewhat premature moment, all the money left to his wife and son went to pay his funeral expenses. A short time after, the lad's mother died, and the property had to be mortgaged to pay for her obsequies; consequently when his grandmother retired from the struggle within the year, he became a pauper.

One may owe money in China, but the dead may not bury their dead and the debt of funeral extravagance must be discharged at once by the living.

I recall visiting a mausoleum in Canton where dead people of wealth were lying in state prior to removal for burial.

Many of them had lain there for months in spite of the exorbitant prices charged for the use of the mausoleum, and the magnificent coffins in which they reposed, covered with lacquer an eighth of an inch thick had cost, as I was informed, from £300 to £500 each!

Wha-lin-ping had formerly been a military post of some importance garrisoned by fifty soldiers, but its glory had long since departed, and there were now but fourteen. Asked where they were, the villagers waved their hands towards the cabbages. "Tilling the fields"! they said. So these agricultural warriors had metaphorically beaten their sword blades into plough-shares!

However, on the approach of any important functionary they were still hastily summoned, and, donning their unfamiliar tunics, sallied out to meet the great man and escort him the requisite distance, before retiring again to their manure heaps.

Another pestilence from which the country suffers severely is sacred mountains — though there is this much good in them, that here the forests are protected. Every village, unless it is situated right down on the plains, boasts at least one, and Wha-lin-ping was no exception.

Nobody is allowed to molest animal life on these hallowed spots, for all animals found there are hallowed also—for the time being, when they leave the mountain, whether temporarily or permanently, they do so at their own risk, since at they once become mundane again.

With a view to becoming sacred, if only for a fleeting hour, I ascended this mountain with a gun one day, but I had not gone far when a man rushed out of the trees and said such a lot of very profane things, that it was obvious I had mistaken my vocation: whereupon I returned to earth quick.

Though prepared only for summer weather we nevertheless now resolved to ascend the mountains behind Wha-lin-ping and spend a few days in the rhododendron forest. A small wooden temple, some three thousand feet above the village and two thousand feet below the summit of the ridge, seemed a fitting place in which to camp, and thither we repaired on 14th June.

The temple raised on a small level clearing in the forest, was

THE TIBET ROAD

a well ventilated shanty which only partially excluded the rain, and was now deserted, one or two priests remaining in residence only when it was in demand as a popular resort for the burning of incense and asking of favours, during the sixth moon. The valley lay almost at our feet, for the ascent had been very abrupt, and the little village clustered above the deep ravine where the torrent flowed seemed but a stone's throw away; however rain fell in torrents every night, and we felt the cold severely, even after the quite moderate warmth of the valley.

From our platform beneath the summit, we looked across ridge after ridge of dark forest, to a tremendous range of peaks stretching across the western sky, from the great glittering snow-fields of which crept a dozen glaciers, jammed themselves into the black gullies which scarred the mountain face from top to bottom, and spread far down into the valleys.

It was the rainy season, and towards nightfall these towering white peaks presented an ever changing panorama of rock and snow, banded with gleaming cloud where the rays of the setting sun played.

Now the clammy night-mist came pouring in a mighty cascade over the pass into the valley, where it lay for a time heaving, smoking fitfully at the edges, while the stars twinkled lazily in the brief twilight, and the gaunt precipices, draped in snow, rose straight up from the pale ocean of mist to meet them, clear cut against the fading tinges of sunset.

Now long lapping billows of cloud came thundering silently up the mountain side, hungrily licking the dark tree tops as they swept ahead, blotting out the star-lit heaven, and masking the distant peaks behind a seething flood of mist. Only the valleys below were filling with purple light now, and the lower mountains over against the little village were stealthily changing from blue to purple and from purple to black as the shadows deepened.

Thus it remained for a minute or two and then the tide was rolling and swirling out again, leaving crag and glacier and tree-clad ridge yet more sharply silhouetted against the after-glow, where the sky was still dyed with filmy green and turquoise blue, with rose and the deepening purple of night, the magic colours there, of the eternal west.

From Wha-lin-ping, a descent of nearly four thousand feet brought us to the main valley through which foamed the muddy waters of the T'ung-ho to join the Ya-ho above Kiating-fu. It is a considerable river, but quite unnavigable, except for the coracles of the tribesmen, which are in use higher up.

For two days the route lay northwards up the main valley, crossing the river at Liu-ding-chiao by a chain bridge eighty yards long and of uncertain stability.

On the third day we left the T'ung-ho and turned due west into a narrow defile from the mouth of which a boisterous cataract, the Ta-tsien-lu river, rattled into the big valley. Single rope bridges of twisted bamboo strands stretched across this river here and there, the people suspending themselves by thrusting their legs through stout rings and hauling themselves across hand over fist; it must have been hard work when they got to the middle, for the bridges sagged dreadfully.

In eighteen miles we ascended 3100 feet up this tributary and late in the afternoon of 21st June, found ourselves at Ta-tsien-lu.

On retracing our footsteps a fortnight later, we made a brief halt at Loa-si-kow, a small village situated at the junction of the Ta-tsien-lu river with the T'ung-ho. However the deep valley, here 5300 feet above sea level, is almost a desert, its bare granite slopes covered with cactus bushes and little else. There was in fact a drought in the land, and rain-processions were being held daily.

For this purpose a string of youths scantily clad in bathing drawers, with wreaths of willow twined around their heads, paraded the street waving a large willow branch in one hand and a bucket of water in the other.

Then everybody sluiced everybody else, till the street ran with water, and having, with siren-like cajolery, induced stray wayfarers into the shallows, they turned on them and rent them with the dregs.

It looked a delightfully cool job, for there was a breeze like a sirocco coming up the valley at the time. The whole display was certainly conducted in a particularly good tempered and hilarious manner, for the sunny street rang with laughter and the splash of water.

As a rule, a crowd praying for rain is as rough a mob as one can meet with in China, and the appearance of any unusual apparition, such as a foreigner, is at once hailed as the cause of the distress, and becomes a fruitful source of riot.

After this water carnival the recognised course of action is to visit the temple to the rain god and pray humbly enough for rain. If this has no effect, the egregious little god is taken down from his pedestal and put out in the sun to bake, just to show him what it is really like, and when he is cooked to the point of gasping for air, he is restored to his shady corner, and given another chance to behave himself.

But the jurisdiction of the gods is strictly local, for after recrossing the high watershed between the T'ung-ho and the Ya-ho, everybody was praying for a cessation of rain: it had done nothing but rain since we passed that way five weeks before, and even Ching-chi-hsien had got wet this time.

During three days spent at the village of Hwang-ni, already referred to, it rained eighteen hours out of every twenty-four. The people were moist but cheerful. It never did anything else there, they said, so they were not perturbed.

Even at Yung-ching-hsien, fifteen hundred feet lower down the valley, and right away on to Ya-chow at the foot of the mountains, it had rained steadily for five weeks. But they had a remedy here, since they could shut the north gate of the city to stop it, when they got tired; at least they said so.

Till one has wrangled over the point with a Chinaman it is difficult to see how shutting any gate is going to affect the precipitation of rain; after that it becomes quite lucid.

"Shutting the north gate won't help the rain a bit," you exclaim, scoffing.

"It will if you keep it shut long enough," is the reply.

"But it wasn't shutting the gate that stopped the rain," you retort afterwards, somewhat mortified.

"How do you know? It all helps!" replies John.

And there you are, stranded with the hopeless task of proving a negative, or, as an alternative, retiring from the discussion.

Personally, I would retire, and allow them to go on shutting the north gate; after all it doesn't do anybody any harm.

This puts me in mind of a Chinaman who was deploring to a certain missionary the fact that the summer was going to be a particularly long and hot one.

"How do yow know that?" inquired the missionary. "Why, there is an intercalary sixth moon (July) this year."

"But that won't make the summer any longer or hotter, man!"

"Why ever not?" persisted the Celestial. "Isn't the sixth moon very hot, and aren't two moons longer than one?" Logic which goes to the root of the matter as pointedly as that, deserves to succeed.

One of the mules having foundered in the slippery mud and rain of the last march, we were delayed in Ya-chow for a day,

THE TIBET ROAD

while coolie labour was hired to carry the broken down mule's load to the capital.

The rains had now ceased, and covering eighty miles in three days through the withering heat of the plains, where now even the superb white and crimson lotus flowers which smothered the ponds with colour looked limp, we took chairs on the last day, and got back to the capital on 22nd July.

11

TA-TSIEN-LU

TA-TSIEN-LU is a quaint old city 8,400 feet above sea level, crammed into a deep hollow at the junction of three gorge like valleys, and overshadowed by the stupendous peaks of the Mantze country, which frown down upon the pigmy nest from altitudes ranging up to 23,000 feet.

Three incomplete walls pierced by as many gates partially block these valleys, but the cliffs pressing closely upon the city to east and west, are themselves as closed doors. The turbulent little river dashes through the middle of the city, sometimes carrying pieces of it away, for the riparian owners have not seen fit to undertake very extensive bunding operations.

The wooden houses with gray tiled roofs, are built in the Chinese style, but show sufficient evidence in their detailed structure of an extraneous origin; while carved gables, lintels, and window frames testify to the wealth of the city.

Numerous shops, kept for the most part by Chinamen, display a variety of skins and manufactured goods from the interior, but the population which throngs the extremely narrow and dirty streets, is a floating one, composed of nomads sampling city life, Tibetan traders from Lhasa and Anterior Tibet, and tribesmen from the Mantze states.

Ta-tsien-lu may justly be called the last city in China, for we

TA-TSIEN-LU

are now in the Mantze marches, the country of semi-savage tribes, who acknowledge fealty to none save to their own chiefs.

Here cultivation ceases; here is the last city eastwards to which the Indian rupee and the wares of Lhasa find their way; it is the terminus for coolie transport from China, and the starting point for the ula system of travelling, and yet a change has gradually taken place in these forbidding mountains during the past three years, and China is at last making strenuous efforts to extend her authority westwards in substance rather than in name alone, as hitherto.

For this purpose Chao-er-f'eng, brother of the Viceroy of Szechwan, marched through Ta-tsien-lu in 1909 at the head of a considerable body of troops, and is now established far up in Outer Tibet, pacifying the country.

Since the sacking of the monasteries, even the truculent lamas are beginning to fear the strong arm behind the gun, and some of the weaker states are already cowed into submission. It is this territory, so long the sport of both Lhasa and Peking, both of whom it has openly flouted and defied, that China now proposes to make into a new province with Batang as its capital; but that it will continue to be a thorn in the side of the Imperial Government for some time to come, is certain. That such grave events as are now going on in the Mantze country can be carried on in such complete secrecy is one of the marvels of the day. The eyes of Europe are riveted on Tibet, and see nothing, and China, pitied, petted China is teaching the chancelleries of Europe how to carry on a war in silence. The overwhelming irony of it all is delightful to contemplate. Ostensibly we occupied rooms at an inn during our brief stay in the city, but actually we were by day the guests of Mr. and Mrs. Herbert of the China Inland Mission, to whom we were indebted for many a pleasant hour of civilization, as well as for much advice and help in making our hunting arrangements. Their nearest white neighbours were at Ya-chow, eight days' journey distant, and we caught a brief glimpse of the work these good Samaritans undertook, when a man who had opened his leg with an axe, was carried in.

This fellow, being alone in the mountains at the time, had managed to crawl several li after the accident, and had then lain in his home for a month, without hope or comfort, racked with fever, starving and filthy, his leg slowly rotting. When at last he requested his friends to take him to the mission house, he was beyond description, but there he was washed and put to bed, was fed on the very best that could be obtained, and when I saw him later, his leg, in the terrible putrid condition brought on by acute blood-poisoning, had been skilfully dressed by a man who had had no medical training. And the patient was grateful.

Why had he not appealed to the mission sooner? That is the supreme difficulty which the missions have to face out west — a native will not, often cannot, bring fresh blood to them; at present they appeal to the missionary only as a last resource, or maybe after travelling many days, and consequently a fresh wound is almost a novelty to him.

Four out of five cases which apply to the mission in Ta-tsien-lu are surgery cases — stabbing, frost-bite, and mishap with axe or gun, nor is it an easy matter for a man not trained as a surgeon to dress a bad wound freshly made; but when it is weeks old and has been plastered with mud to staunch the flow of blood, the task becomes almost superhuman.

Yet we were assured by Dr. Smith that this man's leg would probably be saved and the wound heal, a verdict which also says a good deal for the extraordinary recuperative powers of the native.

Though Ta-tsien-lu is only a ting or military city, being as already suggested on the frontier of western China, the official is nevertheless an er-fu, that is of prefectural rank, and an official of consequence.

Having known Dr. Smith several years previously in Hsian-fu, he called on us at the mission two days after our arrival, and took afternoon tea, quite at his ease. He is a pleasant man of middle age, friendly to foreigners so long as they let him alone, and, as far as one can judge, conscientious in the discharge of his duties.

Another figure-head in the city is the King of Kia-la, a tribal autocrat, commonly known as the Min-cheng-si, whom we visited at his summer palace, ten miles up the valley.

His Majesty is a puny kinglet however, being completely at the beck and call of the yamen, and not wishing to see us, he shammed ill, though bidding his satellites entertain the unwelcome guests.

His summer palace resembled nothing so much as a mediocre inn, but boasted as one of its fixtures a stone bath supplied with water from a hot spring, an article de luxe with which few native inns are furnished.

Entering the palace was an ordeal at which any man not a dog-fancier might have quailed, for immediately eighteen chains, fastened at intervals of a few feet round the courtyard, were stretched to their utmost, and struggling at the end of each was a dog.

The noise was appalling, the deep baying of the mastiffs mingled with the sharp yelping of the lesser breeds indicating that if any of the chains were to give way, it would be most unwholesome to remain in the neighbourhood. Eight or ten other dogs of gentler disposition were strewn loose round the courtyard, but these only scowled at us as we passed, sniffed superciliously, and resumed their occupation of sleeping, while we went on to the wash-house. The water here was quite pure and just bearably hot, though where it issued from the ground fifty yards distant it was scalding; so we wallowed in the King's bath and came out salmon pink.

We rode back on ula mules, commandeered from some unfortunate wild man through the Yamen; and uncouth little monsters they were, with an awkward gait which caused them to progress broadside on most of the time; the position reminded one vividly of getting stuck while negotiating a high farmyard pailing.

Ula is a system of relay transport obtaining in Tibet and the Mantze states.

In return for a grant of land along the high roads, the people are required to keep in readiness at fixed post-houses a certain number of transport animals — ponies, mules, yak, or even coolie labour, if none other is available, which are at the service of any official travelling with an ula passport. In the case of foreigners, who however are not legally entitled to the privileges of the system, payment is made at the yamen in the first instance, a passport is obtained, and the traveller is furnished with a fresh set of animals at the end of each day's stage, free of further charge.

Unfortunately, abuse of the system by Chinese officials has tended to make it both uncertain in design and unsatisfactory in execution, though theoretically it is an excellent, indeed the only possible method to adopt, in these unsettled wilds.

The city was a place of surprises. It was on this jabbering, slouching crowd of the strangest people on earth, which ebbed and flowed listlessly through the narrow streets, that the Chinese shopkeepers, like parasites of Machiavellian cunning, grew fat.

Amongst this motley throng were tall, bony men, wrapped in greasy skins, who lived their lives in the saddle, with the terrible rigours of nomadic life in the mountains stamped on their hard-lined faces, bringing musks; derelicts from the monasteries sacked during the recent fighting, bringing wonderful paintings and idols saved from the wreckage; pilgrims from Lhasa; yak herdsmen taking out the tea brought in on the backs of Chinese coolies; and strange primitive men, with nothing save their hardy ponies and long guns.

One day I was confronted by a stalwart tribesman with a most undisciplined coiffre, and an adequate wardrobe which in parts seemed to cling to him with obvious reluctance.

As he passed, he doubled himself up like a foot-rule, while at the same time, a black, cavernous opening, shaped something like a laterally compressed soup tureen, spread slowly across his copper-brown face, and from the depths of it there jutted out a soup-ladle without the bend in it.

I felt incensed. "Insolent tribesman," I thought, "you may grin from ear to ear, and waggle your tongue at me, but I treat you with haughty disdain..."

At this moment I remembered that the dear old freak was paying me the highest compliment he knew, and I fled in disorder. It was the Tibetan salute.

Many of the Mantze girls look extremely pretty, tricked out with heavy silver bangles, ear-rings, and necklaces of coral or turquoise.

Of course that is not all. Dark blue skirts hitched up behind and hide boots reaching to the knee, give them an Amazonian appearance which is rather enhanced by the coils of black hair, closely interwoven with strands of crimson twine, bound turban-wise round their heads, and the handsome, open face with its large dark eyes, from which the light flashes and dances when they smile. Yes, it is a great relief to see women in skirts again; we may be slaves to convention, but it leaves one with a terrible sense of loneliness and abandonment to be set free.

Yet distance lends enchantment to the view in the case of

these swarthy beauties, and it is only fair to add that this pious opinion is reciprocal.

It is a platitude amongst the Tibetans, that if a man needs to wash himself every day, he must be extremely dirty. They do not wash every day — in fact, they never do so at all, the nearest they ever get to it being to butter themselves well, as their mothers buttered them on the day they were born, before putting them out in the sun to dry. Therefore — but here is the weak spot in an otherwise able syllogism — therefore, they cannot be dirty.

It looks like a postulate standing on its head, but the delicious candour of logic such as this must make the stereotyped logician ashamed of himself, and, by drawing his sting, render concise reasoning a blunt weapon.

Cleanliness is next to godliness; but what an unconscionable amount of time the latter must absorb, since there is no time at all for the former!

A mile from the city was the lamasery and having obtained permission to visit it one morning, we were escorted there by a friendly lama, and introduced to a very portly person of high degree, the sacristan perhaps.

We were rather astonished to hear from our lama friend that he had a son in Germany, engaged as tutor of the Tibetan language to a young German.

Viewed from the outside the temple itself was neither very big nor very imposing, but the exterior was a very misleading index to the splendour of the interior, for it is amazing, the sources of wealth tapped by even the most squalid looking lamasery, and the treasure stored away or exhibited in the form of brazen images, would beggar the mines of Ophir.

In this temple, the great Buddha seated on his gorgeous throne measured seven feet from the base of the pedestal to the top of the crown, and was solid brass, plated with gold, and in many places

TA-TSIEN-LU

thickly crusted with precious stones — rubies, pearls, turquoise, and coral. In front of the altar, four immense bronze urns, each capable of holding 365 pounds of butter, now half spent, — a pound for every day in the year, guarded the sacred butter flames which had burned, perhaps, thus for centuries, and other tiny butter lamps flickered dimly everywhere, casting wavering rays which hovered here and there amongst the recesses of the temple, to be soon swallowed up in the gloom. Small figures made from tsamba, a kind of Tibetan bread, and little dishes of cereals, stood on the altar, and though these offerings do not appear to diminish very rapidly in quantity, they are always presented to the gods. An exciting incident occurred while we were examining the treasures of the temple, for some facetious priest let loose the big mastiff which guarded the sacred precincts, and he came dashing in like a small circus pony, vengeance in his blood-shot eyes, and murder in his heart.

There was a hasty scramble for back seats, and a big pillar being conveniently near, I quickly vanished behind it, while the lama and the portly gentleman, immune from violence, faced the furious dog.

It was quite a pretty little encounter, for not till the stubborn brute had been hit across the face again and again as he charged, did he slink out growling, only half convinced that we had any business on his beat.

A request was now tendered to the Min-cheng-si to allow us to go out in the direction of his summer palace and spend a few days at work amongst the wooded mountains which enclosed the valley higher up, the Chinese official being also informed of our plans.

The King's answer, which however did not reach our ears directly, but took the form of a policy of evasion, was in reality a curt refusal, whereupon our friend the official stepped in, and intimated to him that not only must he make full arrangements for our reception, but he was to see to everything we wanted.

Not wishing to offend his patron (who doubtless could have made things very unpleasant for him), he reluctantly acceded to our request, and two days later we went out to a small Mantze hut, situated half a mile from the palace at an altitude of 10,000 feet. The Min-cheng-si, more ever, so far carried out his instructions as to send round his card and greetings, together with a present of food, though he himself kept discreetly in the background, and pretended to be ill the whole time we were in the neighbourhood.

The reason for his inhospitable attitude was not difficult to fathom, since he regarded us very much in the nature of tramps or gypsies, — and no one could deny that that was exactly what we looked like.

It is an axiom that only beggars walk in Tibet. Amongst the present of victuals was a kettle of tea made in the style peculiar to the country — that is, with butter and salt, though the Min-cheng-si, being averse to rancid butter, we were spared that horror. However, it was a most nauseating beverage, — drunk out of a tea cup. But so much does the association of ideas control our likes and dislikes, that on pouring it into a plate and taking it with a spoon as though it were soup, I was forced to reverse my former verdict. Mocked in this way, it was a distinctly palatable mixture.

We were now comfortably installed in the cottage of our Mantze host, and though unable to exchange a word with either him or his wife, neither of whom spoke Chinese, they were nevertheless very affable in dumb show. In the city it was no uncommon thing to find men, whether Tibetan, Mantze, or Chinamen, speaking the three languages fluently, but no sooner did one get away from the melting pot, than the Chinese was quickly lost.

It rained most of the time we were here, both day and night, and during ten days we had only one clear day, affording an uninterrupted view of the inimitable mountains which rose on every hand.

To see these in all their overwhelming glory, it was of course necessary to climb out of the deep valley in which we were situated, and this particular day being singularly favourable, I ascended to an altitude of 16,000 feet, not far below the snow line. Here, beyond the limit of tree growth, with only dwarf rhododendron scrub, and a wealth of brilliant alpine flowers on every hand, I obtained such a view of snowfield, cornice, and glacier as turns the soul to water as one gazes. Right above my head towered the crest of the mountain, an ugly black ridge jagged and forbidding, running steeply upwards to where the snow clung in dazzling sheets of spotless white.

From out of the couloir facing me, where the snow slopes ended, spread a glacier, not big, but slashed across with crevasse after crevasse, the spot where it plunged over a short precipice marked by a melee of drunken, tottering seracs, their icy cleavage faces flashing and glittering in the noonday sun.

I looked below, a thousand feet below from the flower spangled ridge on which I stood, into the barren rock-strewn gully, with its bare gray piles of moraine stuff heaped up everywhere.

From the wonderful blue ice-caves at the foot of the glacier, thundered a milky torrent, and crashed heedlessly amongst the rocks; the wild noise floated up gently on the wind.

Far away to the south, another range of giants had flung back the caressing cloud wreaths which again and again formed slowly round them, as a woman might fling off a shawl, to stand out bold and unsullied in the perfect panorama.

To the north, Ta-tsien-lu had sunk out of sight in a tiny hollow, overshadowed by purple hills, and westwards the Batang road could be seen, threading its way over range beyond range, till it wound out of sight in the dancing haze.

Over all, a dead silence, save for the muffled roar of the glacier river, rising, falling, dying out, again rising as the wind comes up; above, the blue sky and the everlasting snow; and then, cutting through the tense silence like a meteor, the sharp, incisive crack of an ice pillar, and a curious noise, difficult to locate, as the fragments go sliding and rattling into the gully. It is magnificent, for here the mightiest forces of nature are at work unheeded.

12

Omi-San

THE SUMMER exodus from the capital had long set in when we finally left the shelter of its walls on 26th July.

There was now plenty of water in the Min river, and we drifted easily down stream, still in the fertile country of the red basin, the mountains to the south presently showing up plainly on the horizon. The ninety odd miles to Kiating-fu were covered in two days, but the mission houses in that city also were silent and deserted, though H.M.S. Woodlark was alongside the ramshackle bund, for Kiating marks one of the limits to the radius of action of the British Navy.

The Ya-ho from the north-west, which we had already crossed at Ya-chow, here joins the Min, swelling its flood considerably, the city standing in the apex of the angle thus formed, fronting both rivers.

Seen from the Ya-ho, it presents a picturesque appearance of white gabled houses alternating here and there with clump of bananas, palms, and other semi-tropical vegetation, all rising from behind red sandstone walls which, however, are little visible, for the soft crumbling stone is deeply corroded by the dust storms which sweep across the plain, and has long ago given root-hold to masses of shrubs and creepers which everywhere hang in bunches over it; altogether a charming background of

ON THE ROAD TO TIBET

soft blended colouring to the murky waters of the Ya-ho. Indeed it is surprising what aesthetic spots there are in China, restful to the eye, but odious and abhorrent to almost all the other senses. Not that Kiating is a particularly obnoxious city, but merely that, like many another pearl of Szechwan, its beauty, seen from a distance, is so very much more pronounced than its perfume, say, contrariwise, that its perfume, in situ, is so very much more pronounced than its beauty; which proves the natural cussedness of things.

A high bluff of red sandstone, crowned by a canopy of trees from amongst which peeps up the curling gray roof of a temple, and the old guardian pagoda of the city, like nearly all the pagodas of Szechwan, bulging in the middle of its height and tapering at both ends, here forms the east bank of the Min river; across the Ya-ho, to west and south, stretches the Kiating plain, terminating in the mountains which fringe the Lolo country; and right in the fore-ground, rising abruptly from the plain with no unnecessary frills in the way of foothills clinging to its skirts, is Omi-san, the most sacred mountain in China.

Omi has probably been an object of awe ever since man first climbed its giant cliffs, and looked down in superstitious terror at the picture which has made it famous throughout eastern Asia; but apart from that, its peculiar aspect, stupendous precipices, and convenient situation right on the edge of the great and populous plain of Kiating, fully entitle it, in Chinese eyes, to be invested with sacred properties.

The hard working pedestrian will find the stage from Kiating to Omi-hsien quite sufficient for one day, at least during the hot weather though twenty-four miles does not sound a great deal; the chair-bearers, however, usually take one as far as the temple known as Ta-wu-su, situated on the lower slopes of the mountain, in one day, though this entails abandoning the greater part of one's kit for the night.

Omi-hsien, a small but busy city which obviously owes its air of smug respectability and prosperity to the native pilgrims, who pass through it from the four corners of China, lies almost due west of Kiating on the small Omi river, at the foot of the mountain.

It boasts some of the dirtiest inns I have ever seen in Szechwan, and a local breed of mosquitos which would suck blood from a knight in armour.

However we survived the night, and reached Ta-wu-su, 3,000 feet above sea level, on the following morning.

Here some twenty pilgrims, travelling incog, from Ya-chow, Cheng-tu, Kiating and intermediate hsiens, in search, not of merit, but of a holiday, greeted us with great cordiality, and we realized for the first time what a very nice place a Buddhist temple can be so long as it is not prostituted to unworthy objects.

Ta-wu-su is not sufficiently elevated to be cool, but being a commodious temple, conveniently near Omi-hsien, from where supplies must be drawn, yet above the sweltering miasmas of the plain, it forms the headquarters of most parties summering on the mountain.

It is now a sort of rambling old hotel, on the pavilion system, rather than a temple; a terrace has been profained into an excellent asphalt tennis court (and also a sort of back yard in which to hang the clothes on washing day), though the sedate old priests must think people crazy to run about on a hot afternoon, hitting a ball over a net; and if religious orgies made one sometimes court sleep in vain, we retaliated on Sunday evenings (though at a more legitimate hour), attracting quite a crowd of gray-gowned Buddhists to the tennis court, eager to hear the rival religion under full steam.

This neutralization of the temples on Omi, indicates that,

what with government schools and, so to speak, family hotels, these cumbersome buildings of little interest and less beauty, are at last being put to some use; when I see a Buddhist temple converted into a railway station, I shall begin to have genuine faith in the future of railways in China.

For the two days we stayed at Ta-wu-su, we were the guests of Dr. and Mrs. Shields of Ya-chow, who would not hear of our setting up house on our own account — which was just as well, seeing that the apartments were let unfurnished; meanwhile we paid calls on the inhabitants of other suites in the temple.

Across one of the deep valleys which gutter the mountain on the Kiating side, and so up over the next ridge, lies the slope known as Shing-kai-su, where five or six bungalows have been built at intervals of half a mile or less by the Kiating people, forming another small colony. Being a good thousand feet higher than Ta-wu-su, on a ridge from which both the summit and the plain are visible, its situation is an improvement on the nest in which the temple lies; but of course the companionship which makes the latter so jolly, is comparatively absent. For the recluse, or the hermit who can sit and dream that things are not what they seem, for the invalid who needs rest and quiet, for the first year of married life, or any other similar situation bursting with silent bliss, Shing-kai-su is a paradise; but for the boisterous spirits so long pent up under the great atmospheric pressure of the plains, — well, I am neither a recluse nor a hermit, nor an invalid myself nor am I in imminent peril of getting married. The summit of Omi may be reached from Ta-wu-su by either of two roads, which diverge at a spot known as Flying Bridges, not far distant. The responsibility for this name rests with the temple, and is not derived from any inherent tendency to aviation in the bridges themselves, which span a picturesque gorge in a very orthodox and motionless manner.

What is called the small road ascends one of the trench-like valleys, its steep flanks all softened and smothered by the luxuriant vegetation, crosses, a ridge into the next parallel valley, passing Chiu-lou-tung under the shadow of a vast cliff, descends across this, valley and up on to the next ridge, where it joins the big road which has simply followed this ridge up from below, and so skirting along the edge of the precipices facing Kiating, to the summit.

A good walker can reach the summit from Ta-wu-su by either route in a day, but it is distinctly preferable to take two over it.

Leaving Ta-wu-su, we chose the small road and went as far as Chiu-lou-tung, nearly half way to the top, climbing an enormous number of steps in order to account for a descrepancy of some four thousand feet of altitude. This temple we made our headquarters for a week, and it was delightfully cool up here.

Chiu-lou-tung, though not much to look at, being the usual pine shingle jerry-built cabin with a sheet lead roof, is one of the most famous temples on the mountain, chiefly on account of the cave, which gives its name to the place.

It must have, in fact, an Asiatic reputation, since money for the pagoda they were now preparing to erect (on free trade principles) had been sent from t'ien-chiu-kuei, wherever that may be, — the "land beyond Burma," as the head priest informed us; it is a delightfully vague designation for a place.

Wood for the pagoda was being cut from the forests of fir and Arancaria, stone quarried from the limestone cliffs, and every pilgrim who was unable to subscribe cash was expected to put his back into an afternoon's work, log rolling, or, like Sisyphus, bundling stones up a hill. There was no conspicuous slump in the labour market.

Caves always seem to me very much over-rated places of amusement. The only justification they have for existing, is as the haunts of pirates and genii, who generously find it incumbent on them to use such mysterious places as convenient chancery establishments, leaving a nice obvious clue appraising a romantic posterity of the fact.

This one was vested instead with all kinds of weird holiness, being a great favourite with the pilgrims who daily arrived in swarms to see what they could extract from a grudging galaxy of gods, though the mendicant season was now far advanced.

It started down hill at a great pace, but was fairly lofty, though occasionally it became necessary to duck one's head to avoid breaking the beautiful stalactites which were heard rather than seen, — heard and felt, dripping like a burst water pipe; and throughout, it would have been conducive to one's comfort to have carried an umbrella, out of respect for the thousands of bats and swallows which covered the roof with a living mosaic, and darted wildly up and down the passages. The route was flag-marked conspicuously enough by forests of incense sticks, which formed bunches of glowing red spots in the deep gloom every few yards, filling the damp cave with stifling columns of smoke and apparently inconveniencing the denizens of the roof, for they ceased after a time; and then at a turn in the path a hundred yards from the entrance perhaps, and deep down in the cliff, we came suddenly upon the treasure trove, looking very tarnished behind the film of smoke. There was the usual altar and a number of hanging lamps and lighted candles, and an aged priest who blinked like an owl; perhaps cave life was turning him into some strange blind creature.

But there was no very formidable janitor grinning beside the entrance to the secret chamber behind the altar, nor did it look so very secret. Indeed, the chief objection to going any further was that one had to crawl down an unhealthy looking passage, which seemed hardly worth while in a cave so devoid of jewels and glitter as this one certainly was.

The subtle incantations and empty sophistries of Chinese Buddhistic worship were now our daily portion, for we could not get away from them.

The day's mede of praise always anticipated the sun, beginning about 3.80 a.m. with a concert remarkable for its lack of rhythm; it insinuated itself stealthily into one's dreams — the lilt of the priestly choir, the rolling cadence of gongs softly pleading, quickly banishing idyllic memories which sleep had conjured up, and substituting gruesome phantoms, till finally, giving place to a drowsy overture of wailing protestation, it acted the part of a perfect soporific, and the sufferer turning over on to the other side, was permitted to resume the thread of his unfinished dream where he had inadvertently dropped it.

The old priest sat at his table half the day, visible to all men, the better for the right hand to see what the left hand did, drumming mechanically on a wooden gong to shut out the noises of the external world, reading the ching, or Buddhist scriptures, with praiseworthy persistence. He always read the same book, and went through it twenty times a day, for he was a very holy man. In the afternoon there would be a sort of choir practice for the assistant priests and apprentices, some of them mere children, who were not yet sufficiently versed in the business to have the nine spots burnt on the head, admitting them into the brotherhood of fully qualified priests.

This was one of the most dismal rehearsals of the day, and it was expedient to contrive to be out while these people, the very rawest of tyros, held the stage.

At nine o'clock came the final spasm, — the beating of the big drum indicating bed time, and the ringing of the big bell by some devout idiot sitting cross-legged in front of it and mumbling away like a moon-struck loon, whacking the bell at intervals.

However it was all over in fifteen minutes or so, and the temple plunged in profound silence and darkness, save for the lamps which burned perpetually before the shrines.

Buddhist temples in China do not compare with the monasteries of Tibet. They are smaller, dingier, and altogether less splendid. Religion is here not a part of life, but a release from its cares. The Buddhist religion in fact, before dying out (and no one will deny that it is on the wane, and at least very lukewarm in eastern Asia) has behaved in the manner of those strange creatures once inhabiting the earth, who, ere they became finally extinct made one desperate rally against the conquerors, breaking out into all sorts of extravagant forms in their attempt to stave off the inevitable hour; then quietly gave up and died. It took aeons, and the passing of Buddhism may take generations, but the hand-writing is on the wall.

What could be more grotesque than the several sects of Lamaism! Compare them with the aberrant Buddhism of China, with its appearance of sulky adherence to the letter and indolent combativeness to the spirit of Guatama's creed, or with the faded magnificence of Burma and the south. Besides the central Buddha, resplendent with gold paint, occupying the front of the temple, there were five subsidiary groups of immortals behind, and stretching down the short length of the building, two rows of Buddha's disciples, nine on either side — almost life sized figures, raised three feet above the floor on a shelf, most of them in a sitting attitude, reminding one somewhat of the Temple of the Five Hundred Genii, in Canton.

These disciples of Buddha vary in almost every temple, but certain conventional attitudes, expressions, and pieces of apparel seem to always recur, so that anyone acquainted with Chinese Buddhism may be able to recognise the gentlemen concerned from the following brief descriptions of them which I jotted down.

Left side of the central group.

Number one holds a book in one hand, while the other is raised in a mildly deprecating fashion, a look of benign simplicity on his vacant face.

Number two has one knee drawn up, his hands clasped round it. His lined countenance is puckered into a look of horrified surprise.

Number three sits bolt upright clasping some bizarre object in his hands, which are held out in front of him. A sour expression pervades a countenance never lovely at the best of times.

Number four sits with an elbow resting on either knee, one hand outspread in an imbecile fashion, the other grasping a bell. Judging by his look of harmless idiocy, his one idea of bliss is to sit there ringing that bell.

Number five is a furious fellow. One leg is drawn up and rests on the head of a cat which smiles indulgently, saying plainly enough: "Why look you, how you storm! I would be friends with you!" The man is only partly clad and holds aloft a ring which he seems about to cast from him. His other hand rests on his hip, and his expressive face is convulsed with unrighteous rage — possibly at the cat's smile.

Number six is another featherhead. On his lap is a frog, rather elongated, which he caresses with one hand, while between the finger and thumb of the other, he delicately clasps a marble, holding it up for inspection.

Number seven is a hypocrite. He clasps his hands in front of him with an air of sublime sanctity, while from behind them the face of a truculent mountebank grins defiance.

Number eight sits with hands clasped in his lap and the air of one enjoying a hot foot-bath, which has stamped an expression of supine contentment on a delightfully plain face.

Number nine is evidently sitting on a pin, and endeavouring, at the expense of great facial distortion, not to let on that it hurts. His knees are crossed, his hands clasped on his lap in resigned martyrdom; only his staring eyes and parted lips betoken the stoical fortitude of the man, and the penetrating power of pins in general.

Eight side of the central group.

Number one is a freak. His eye-brows are serpentine, extending as long streamers to a length of over two feet. With a self-satisfied smile he supports one of them between tapering fingers, his hand resting on his up-drawn knee, while his face betrays his feelings, which may be expressed: "Look at that, my boy"!

Number two is a pious fellow, with hands clasped in front of him as though in prayer. But his face betokens complete indifference to the results cf supplication.

Number three sits with a hand on either knee and a smug air of propriety on his unhandsome face.

Number four has his hands crossed on his lap, and his calm face betokens an optimistic if not a fatalistic mind.

Number five is another hot tempered person, showing a very- dirty set of teeth in a vicious scowl. One hand he waves aloft, as though about to address a public meeting, and in the other he holds half a cocoanut shell, from the centre of which springs a serpent, so that his address probably opens with: "Oh ye generation of vipers!"

Number six is a quiet man, spreading a scroll open on his knees and, with a dry smile, freely inviting people to examine it.

Number seven has recently been interrupted in a speech, and holds up his hand in mild protest, his passive face contracted into a smile.

Number eight is a harmless looking soul, his hands piously

clasped in front of him, where he holds a box of very precious ointment.

Number nine is seated in great comfort with his legs crossed and drawn up under him. His immense paunch, exposed to the vulgar gaze, indicates that he is not in the habit of denying himself the fleshpots of Egypt, but his fat, good humoured face screwed up into the semblance of epicurean appreciation, has a lurking suspicion of tragedy about it, which suggests that he is a slave to dyspepsia.

It was as good as a lesson in manners to watch the pilgrims cautiously endeavouring to remember the proper etiquette of theistic society, which is thoroughly dominated by caste. The rank of each god must be appropriately discriminated — to offend one of them would be a horrid blunder.

The central image first receives his kotows, with wooden indifference that does him credit, considering that the man prostrates himself three times; this nabob also receives the lion's share of the incense.

The waxworks in the rear of the central group, various small satellites and members of the household, are treated with a little less ceremony, and finally the rows of disciples are put off with perfunctory bows and a stick of incense between them; they could do little for him, and the Chinaman does not as a rule spend time and money unless substantial concessions, real or imagined, are guaranteed in return. It was a most illuminating "at home." Some doctrines of this effete form of worship were ruthlessly exposed to us here by the garrulous priests; how the majority of them spent their miserable pittance gambling; how they periodically visited Omi-hsien and squandered what they could on riotous living, wine and — its alliterative attendant.

It was instructive also to compare the various motives which had driven young men to seek the cloth. Several of them freely unbosomed themselves.

In China, it is not the bright boy of the family, nor the student, who aspires to the church.

One youth naively informed us that he had become a priest because he did not care to face the worry and responsibilities of modern business, in which many people barely made a living!

Of several little boys apprenticed to the faculty while mere babies, one, aged nine, found himself an embryonic priest on the death of his parents, because his friends did not wish to be put to the trouble of looking after his welfare; a second, aged twelve, because his parents called in a blind fortune teller who had prophesied concerning him that if he did not become a priest, all kinds of evils would assail him.

The prayers which were mumbled at these festive gatherings were the most utter rubbish.

To wake up before the east was turning gray, and hear these frenzy priests droning the "language of heaven" as it is called, was to ensure such an ebullition of vicious feelings that one instinctively decided to give that golden shore a decided miss in one's travel.

Dub, dub, dub, goes the drum; ba, ba, ba, wong, wong, wong, da, da, da, bong, bong, bong, droned the chorus, keeping time like a board school singing class.

Then suddenly, silence for one ecstatic moment, while the head priest goes on by himself, like the vicar when he reads the Litany.

These ridiculous noises making up the language of heaven are each represented by a character, and all are written in a book, to be learnt by heart, though they mean absolutely nothing.

However we may console ourselves with the thought that if we ever meet in heaven, such a monosyllabic language should present few conversational difficulties.

13

OMI-SAN — (CONTINUED)

BEFORE LEAVING finally Chiu-lou-tung we made a journey of exploration to the top of the mountain in order to discover other hunting grounds higher up.

Eventually we decided in favour of a small temple about a thousand feet below the summit, and thither we repaired on 18th August; it was to be our last locality before starting on our long journey to the coast.

In spite of the dense vegetation which made big game hunting impossible, even had the priests granted us permission to use firearms, we obtained more species of small animals on Omi-san than in any other single locality, and almost doubled the total number of specimens in a month; moreover several of these new animals were complete novelties in the zoological world, so that we finished up with a satisfying feeling of work successfully accomplished.

Meanwhile some of our Canadian friends had come up from below to spend a week on the summit.

It was a hard hour's climb from our temple to the top, but I never found it too much trouble to go up and spend the afternoon with this jolly family.

Dr. Shields was paterfamilias to all and sundry (we were the sundries) and he may well have had his hands full, for the Canadian girls, of whom there were five in the party, are a spirited lot, just as brimful of genuine fun when on a holiday, as of genuine work when in harness, and we had any amount of good times together.

The summit of Omi also offers some of the most remarkable sights imaginable, not the least astonishing of which is the view, occasionally to be obtained, of the snow mountains of Tibet, south of Ta-tsien-lu, distant more than a hundred miles.

Seen in the first flush of dawn, suffused with a pink glow as the sun rises over the Kiating plain, they seem on fire; no longer are they snow mountains, but burning craters, the glow from which shines through their glassy slopes.

While we look, they are transfigured, blanching rapidly as the sun rises higher, and before mid-day the clouds roll up and obscure them behind massive puffs with gilt edges, piled high one on another.

From amidst this richest cloudland rise two strange table mountains, one of which is called Wa-wa-san.

Both are many miles long, their summits, formerly perhaps, like those whose rounded peaks rise cape beyond cape out of this sunlit sea, now cut clean off with a giant knife as it appears; and the stumps, mutilated but undismayed, not without a wild beauty of their own, planed to a dead level, falling abruptly away in precipices on every hand.

To the south, green mountains streaked with dark gullies full of rich vegetation melt into blue, and the blue hills grow fainter and melt into the summer clouds of the Lolo country, and fade out of sight.

As the harvest moon rises, a great yellow orb seen through the veil of mist hanging over the plain, the rim of the snow mountains again becomes outlined, till at last, under the glare of the moon now riding undimmed, high up in cloud less space,

OMI-SAN—(CONTINUED)

they glitter all across the western horizon. So quiet and peaceful is it, so alike are sights and scenes under the softening and muffling pall of night, that this might be the Alps from Geneva, instead of the savage barriers of Tibet.

All these pictures we watch unrolling before us from the balcony of the temple crowning the huge cliff which stands boldly out like a headland, washed at its base by the imaginary Kiating sea, now a sea of yellow rice and cornfields, so far below that no sound of breaking waves could ever come up to us.

Though the glory of this temple was destroyed more than three centuries ago, never to be restored, pieces remain to testify to its ancient beauty — two miniature pagodas, about fifteen feet high, exquisitely chaste, parts of the bronze altar, studded with carving, and a few other relics. For the famous bronze temple was destroyed by lightning during the sixteenth century.

But the most wonderful sight lies right at our feet, beneath the balcony, where yawns that fearful abyss, the steep ridges green with forest trees, which buttress the great cliff dipping down, down, two thousand feet to the silvery wisps of mist hanging in mid air, and down beyond them to the rolling country, and still down between the spreading capes out on to the wide Kiating plain stretching to the horizon, across, which crawl a whole mapful of twisting rivers.

Towards the middle of a summer afternoon, when the abyss was full of mist, with the sun shining on it from behind, there may be seen the strange apparition which has made Omi-san famous to the borders of India — Buddha's glory.

To a superstitious and devout people, it is a sight wonderful enough, and the crafty priesthood would not be likely to minimise its undoubted splendour; even wise men from the west can hardly point to a more celebrated example of the phenomenon, which however is paralleled by the spectre of the Brocken in the

Hertz mountains.

Put briefly, Buddha's glory consists of a halo of colour, nothing more nor less than a rainbow, in the centre of which appears the outline of a colossal human figure, plainly the shadow of the observer, cast by the sun.

Floating in space from one to three thousand feet or more below the brink of the precipice, the sight may well awe those accustomed to account for anything uncanny by an appeal to supernatural causes; nor is it matter for surprise that in previous days, such was the emotion evoked by the sight, that fanatics were wont to cast themselves over the precipice into the arms of the elusive Buddha awaiting them so far below, only to find, or fail to find, that those arms were not so strong to save as they appeared to the religious suicide.

Unfortunately, I never saw the entire Buddha's glory myself, as all the conditions for its complete display were never satisfied synchronously on my visits to the summit; but of its genuineness there can be no question.

There is yet another remarkable illusion, well-known to visitors on this mountain, but, with incomplete testimony to lay before readers, I hesitate to more than mention it. It is said that on clear nights, strange lights are to be seen from the top of the mountain, away down on the crags, now here, now there, waxing, waning, advancing, retreating, in places absolutely inaccessible to human beings, or even suspended in mid air. So much for traveller's tale.

On two successive nights I was on the summit, looking for these phantom lights; on both occasions there was a brilliant moon, then at the full, rising over the shadowy plain into an almost clear sky, flooding the black mountains of the Lolo country with its cold silver light, and this is what I saw.

Away down out of the blackness, a bright light, of a golden

red colour, suddenly appeared, waned, and went out; another appeared higher up, faint at first, then glowing more brightly, and yet a third, and far across in the next gully came still another, and another, though even when six or seven had been located, rarely were more than one or two seen at the same time.

These lights were large and brilliant, of an unmistakable reddish glow, which came and went with strange ease. They did not change their position however, nor were any of them suspended in mid air; but that some of them show in places where no human habitation existed is certain, though whether those places were literally inaccessible may be doubted. A place may look totally inaccessible from one spot, and yet be comparatively easy of access from another. Yet it must be admitted that the lights were an enigma, for no reasonable explanation will satisfactorily account for them. They are to be explained by no kind of natural phosphoresence, whether of animal or plant origin, and the suggestion that they are the fires of charcoal burners seems to be easily refuted.

In the first place, assuming that they occur in spots readily accessible (a supposition the truth of which I cannot vouch for), charcoal fires are of necessity covered over with turf, columns of smoke would be seen arising from them by day, and the capricious appearance and extinction of the lights is not accounted for.

Moreover some of these lights are to be observed at a distance of several miles, which would hardly be possible in the case of lights displayed in temple or cottage, both of which are usually shrouded in darkness at nightfall.

A third view, namely that the lights are simply reflections of the stars, distorted and magnified by the mist, is easily discounted by several arguments, not the weakest of which is the fact that though the stars undoubtedly twinkle, they do not work in and out like so many aerial concertinas.

ON THE ROAD TO TIBET

But while no rational explanation, so far as I know, has ever been offered of this peculiar occurrence, there is no justification merely on that account for suggesting the intervention of supernatural causes: the phenomenon belongs to the category of the unexplained. Doubtless it is capable of interpretation in simple terms, only such interpretation is still lacking.

Whether the lights do ever appear, like Buddha's glory, in space, and whether they can actually be seen moving about, are moot points which I cannot answer for, never having seen such a miracle; but I have been assured by foreign visitors that such is the case. For me it is sufficient that the lights are actually to be seen on clear nights, and they are *sui generis* sufficiently remarkable.

On 22nd August we started down *en mass*, following the big road down the hog's-back to Ta-wu-su.

Half way down we reached the temple of Wan-yan-su where is concealed a pearl of great price, for the usual pine shingle building, rudely put together, serves to smother the interior of the temple and its appurtenances. Once inside however, we are in a new atmosphere, for the scene has changed abruptly; we are in a brick temple of India, nearly two thousand years old may be. The building is square in shape, with a domed roof; dark, not with the dim religious light of an abbey, which is light enough to inform you that it is full of noble memories, and dark enough to leave you ever in the pursuit of those memories which is better than their attainment, but with that scowling darkness which one unconsciously associates with caves or the black hole of Calcutta; small enough to be tucked away inside the jerry-built product of present day Buddhism in China, thus looking as though it were surrounded by a stick-no-bills London hoarding; large enough to hold a perfect specimen of early Indian workmanship in the form of an elephant upon which rides a Buddha glittering with gold paint, though the elephant itself is black with age and almost invisible till one stands beneath it. Dimensions, like statistics, are the dullest reading in the world, so we need not discuss those of the elephant, especially as they have all been given before. Suffice to say that except for the extremely short and squat legs, it is as large as Jumbo, the famous elephant formerly at the Zoo, and looks it, since it is set on high pedestals which minimise the ridiculous shortness of its legs.

The elephant is of brass, and was cast by Indian workmen who came over for the purpose I don't know how many years ago — perhaps when the Buddhist religion was at its zenith, say in the fifth or sixth century, or perhaps on its introduction into China, during the first century.

It is a remarkable casting, and the workmanship is superb; the only drawback is that it is impossible to see any more than the top of the animal's head; the rest of it can only be outlined with one's hands. It stands in the small vaulted chamber facing the entrance, so that an excellent view of it should be obtained from the front.

Unfortunately a stone paling, about five feet high, rings it round, and effectually blocks out the light from the lower regions, while the rider with his regal howdah nearly as big as the elephant itself, reaching almost to the top of the domed roof (sufficient to break any elephant's back not made of brass), blocks it out from above.

Add to this that the elephant is now black and its burden a rainbow of gold and many colours, and the reason for the invisibility becomes apparent.

Behind, there is no light at all, and not even the outline of the giant pachyderm can be discerned, though I ascertained the fact that he was complete, tail and all.

Just beneath the base of the dome a number of ledges run

completely round the temple, and on these are set row upon row of small brass Buddhas, which evidently once formed a solid glittering frieze to the more sombre gray brick walls, though the present census shows considerable depopulation; pilgrims have probably carried off the majority of them, whether by might or right. Here also we are shown one of the vast number of fragments into which poor Buddha dissociated on his demise — to wit, a tooth.

This is of course only a pleasant myth, unless Buddha was really as large as the effigy in another temple, a little lower down the mountain, where stood a brass figure twenty-five feet high and broad in proportion, with a hand the size of a ham; for the tooth — certainly it was a tooth, and thus far truth was stranger than fiction, bore the strongest resemblance to an elephant's molar.

Whether the brazen colossus was meant to be Buddha or not I can't say, for his features, being somewhere up near the roof, were as usual shrouded in gloom, and indistinguishable without a search-light, which we had forgotten to bring.

We can only hope that if this sacred tooth (which was carefully preserved in a silk bag) had ever adorned the mouth of Buddha, it was removed after that gentleman's lamented death; for it is difficult to see how such a weapon could be removed with anything less than a steam crane.

Of the numerous temples on Omi therefore, these four are well worth a visit; Ta-wu-su, the most comfortable hotel temple, and general headquarters; Chiu-lou-tung, perhaps the greatest favourite with the pilgrims on account of its caves; Kin-ting on the summit, once the bronze temple, from which may be seen the two spectral phenomena already described; and Wan-yan-su, with its records of the time when Buddhism was a power in the land.

OMI-SAN—(CONTINUED)

We got back to Ta-wu-su late in the afternoon, and having all dispersed to remove the traces of mountaineering from our persons as far as possible, were the guests at several convivial gatherings.

After dinner we all collected in one room, thirty of us, for a farewell entertainment; on the morrow we were to set out for Kiating en route for Shanghai, and the Canadians were beginning to disperse to the cities of central Szechwan. For the last time this year the old temple courts of Ta-wu-su would ring and echo to the chorus of the local song, with popular and personal allusions, which we had written in memory of our family trip to the top of Omi.

It was really a splendid entertainment, though we were crammed into the little room. There were songs and recitations, bunting stories, and parlour tricks, the returned party vying with the Ta-wu-su people in putting forward artistes; and it was nearing midnight when the programme was finished.

Next morning we continued the descent, passed through the hsien with its dirt and its sanguinary mosquitos, and after a most trying march through the dreadful heat of the plain, reached Sü-chi, on the small Omi river. Here we hired a boat and floated the remaining distance down the Ya-ho, reaching Kiating just as night came down. And now our troubles were nearly over.

The last days were spent in packing — packing for the last time, and in visiting some caves cut out of the sandstone and used probably as tombs by the aboriginal Mantze tribes who inhabited Szechwan many centuries ago before they were driven westwards, beyond Tanitsienlu. Sarcophagi had been carved out of niches in the walls, but they were empty, and now the caves were the haunts of beggars and of bats, and their history, whatever it may be, has sunk into irredeemable oblivion.

Then the weather suddenly became cooler; signs of autumn

were already in the air. Now the rice was being cut on the plain and the winter crops would shortly be sown, while the water level in the rivers after the fierce summer rains in the mountains was beginning to fall.

So on 28th August we boarded the junk which was to take us to Chung-king, and in a short time, the guardian pagoda of Kiating was only a streak against the gray sky.

14

TWO THOUSAND MILES ON THE YANG-TSE

28TH AUGUST, 1910, was cool and cloudy, and marked an important date in our calendar. A delightful breeze blew through the junk, as we were borne rapidly along on the strong current.

In the red sandstone cliffs opposite Kiating, above the highest flood-mark, were many gods carved out of the rock, some almost rubbed smooth by the ceaseless wear and tear of atmospheric forces, others still standing out sharply in deep relief; one of these painted carvings was twenty-five or thirty feet high, and cut at least a foot into the rock. They too, perhaps, carry us back to the days when the Mantze tribesmen hewed caves out of the cliff, in which to live and bury their dead.

The Ming river broadens out considerably below the city, and long stretches of quiet water, with high, thickly forested cliffs on one side and low country on the other alternate with rapids, where the river contracts again.

A swim alongside of the drifting junk helped to pass a long afternoon which had suddenly become hot and oppressive, and another when we tied up at nightfall gave me an appetite for supper. How rusty one feels on suddenly taking up a new form of exercise after months of heavy work at something else!

Already we had covered sixty miles of our long river voyage, and next morning we were off at day-break. The river, now fully a quarter of a mile across, though it frequently narrowed down again, ran swiftly, and we could hear it foaming over the rocks inshore, and the occasional guttural chorus of a gang of naked perspiring trackers hauling a junk up-stream.

I went overboard for another swim, but the currents were getting very tricky, and having nearly got left behind I soon came aboard again.

At mid-day two high bluffs appeared in front of us, flanking the river, and on the right bank was a big city high up on the cliff; the river, which so far had twisted but little, now seemed to swing sharply round to the left, and it was easy to see that there was a racing current in front of us.

No, our water is red; it has flowed through the sandstone country, the red basin of Szechwan. But this hurrying dancing flood in front of us is yellow. It comes out of the mountains on the right bank, above the city on the bluff, and rolls straight past our river, hardly seeming to notice its presence, and onwards to the sea.

Can this small stream be the mighty Yang-tse? Why, it looks smaller even than the Min!

Yes, it is so. This big city is Sui-fu, situated at the confluence of the waters; here is indeed the mighty Yang-tse, fed now from the glaciers and snow-fields of Tibet.

It is not such an insignificant stream as it appears; though less than three hundred yards in breadth opposite Suifu, the current is tremendous and the depth incredible.

So swift is the current that as it races past, the waters of the Min seem to be banked up, and a sharp line divides the smooth water of the tributary from the rocking waves of the main stream; indeed to the Chinese, the Min is now the main stream, for the big river is no longer called the Yang-tse.

So we glide out of the calm water into the great highway of

China, and looking back, see the walls and highest roofs of Sui-fu perched up on the promontory, with the smooth red stream of the broad Min river curling round from the right, and the troubled yellow water of the narrow river dashing in from in front, a big triangular lake, almost enclosed by high cliffs, being formed where they meet; in a few minutes Sui-fu and the Min river are out of sight, and we are humming down on the bosom of the Yang-tse.

Long gray lines of sharp rocks, tilted on edge, stick up out of the water first on one side then on the other, and the roar of cataracts is never out of our ears.

Sometimes we sail past close to them and see the water foaming over the rapids; at other times we are far out in the middle of the stream, which is often half a mile across. And throughout the voyage the muddy water is boiling up, eddying round, dashing now this way now that, while we speed on to Chung-king, three hundred miles distant. High hills, their slopes covered with scattered trees, bound the river, and though villages are rare, groves of dark orange trees cluster round hut and temple.

It seems almost incredible that this tremendous river, rolling along peacefully between its distant shores, beyond which rise tier after tier of low tree-clad hills, can gather itself more and more together till at last it is able to fling itself suddenly into the mountains and burst through range beyond range the main axes of which run athwart the river.

On 30th August we passed Lu-chou the centre of the salt trade, being not far distant from the brine wells, and after travelling very well on the following day we tied up in the evening only fifteen miles from Chung-king.

The fog bank had barely lifted from the water on the morning of 1st September when Chung-king loomed up through the mist, and the big gray Roman Catholic hospital crowning the bluff at the upper end of the city took definite shape.

Chung-king, though occupying the angle between two big rivers in the conventional way, is situated a little unusually in other respects.

Two ridges, that nearest the river rising to a height of perhaps a hundred feet above the summer level of the river, the second twice that height, extend parallel to the Yang-tse, and terminate at either end in bold bluffs, that at the lower end of the city facing the Kia-ling, a river which we had crossed seven hundred miles higher up, five months previously.

On and between these ridges the city is built, sweeping in the form of a crescent round the inside of a great bend which the river makes at this point.

By far the most striking, though by no means the most extensive view of it is obtained from below, facing the angle of the bluff where it abuts on the two rivers, — a solid mass of building rising tier on tier above the fringe of boats packed closely along the water's edge.

During winter, the water, no longer turbid as it is at present but clear and sparkling, drops at least seventy feet, and even the houses now raised just above the river, seem to be perched high up on the rock.

From the high hills on the other side however, where many of the residents have built bungalows, the city presents quite a different aspect.

Now we can look down on to the rock and follow the big river for some distance both above and below the city, as well as being able to look across the bluff to where the Kia-ling enters with a tremendous rush. It is a rather smaller river than the Min, but more self-assertive, for it sweeps the Yang-tse water before it, having a regular rough and tumble with it before the two can accommodate themselves to one stream.

At night, when the city stretching away up the ridge is pricked out in lights and the river is indistinct, the view recalls the Peak at Hongkong; when the electric light installation is complete and the city ablaze with arc-lamps, it will doubtless be quite a sight from these hills.

But apart from these more distant views, Chung-king enjoys quite a spurious reputation for magnificence.

Its streets dirty and narrow thronged with hurrying coolies carrying water buckets; its noisome rookeries and poisonous smells; its riparian population herded into miserable sties, dark like cave dwellings, propped up above the river on long poles, where the unhealthy drip of water and the ripple of the current beneath the floor boards are the only sounds of the other world which can penetrate through the dark stifling atmosphere; its festering, obscene beggars lying about the steps at the water-gate, dead and dying alike half in and half out of the water; — this is Chung-king. There is no foreign concession; instead, the European quarters form little islands dotted here and there through this slough of squalor.

Thus the Custom-House, Post-Office, and the new electric-light works form one colony just above the river; the Consulates form another on the ridge behind, and the American Methodist Mission hospital and compounds a third, in the centre of the city.

Across the river, where a string of gun-boats lie, are a few foreign hongs, and on the high hills which encircle the fine paved road leading into Kwei-chow, are scattered bungalows.

Just as Cheng-tu is the western seat of learning, so is Chung-king the city of hospitals, and one cannot help wondering whether the Chinese, having realised the benefits to be derived from these establishments and profited by their presence (which latter they emphatically have done, for the three big foreign hospitals here are always full) — one cannot help wondering whether they intend to leave it at that.

Will they continue to accept the charity of doctors and hospitals, without agitating for medical schools and hospitals of their own, where men can be trained to minister to the needs of their own countrymen? If not, the work of the medical missionaries, apart from the temporary alleviation of suffering, is largely thrown away, for it has no educational value.

The Chinese very rightly (though somewhat prematurely) clamour to build and maintain their own railways; then why not their own hospitals, for which the need is at least equally pressing?

But if the unsightliness of Chung-king is very apparent after the enchantment of Cheng-tu, it cannot be denied that as the door by which all goods coming in to, or leaving Szechwan must pass through, it is of even more importance than the capital.

Strange to say, the foreigner is not popular here in official circles, though his works are regarded with greedy eyes; indeed the Chinese attitude is one with which it is impossible to condole, for they would like the golden eggs but can very well dispense with the goose that lays them.

Unfortunately they are not yet in a position to lay fertile ova themselves, and therein they display that hasty temperament which has already been referred to as such a brake on their rate of progress.

Would they but once learn thoroughly from their teachers, learn even to surpass them, they could very well stand alone; but their dogged antipathy to acknowledging other peoples' superiority makes strangely half-hearted pupils of them.

The standpoint from which the Chung-king officials view foreigners is neatly summed up in a remark attributed to the Taotai.

"I don't mind their gospel," he is reported to have said, "but I can't stand the wretched foreigners"!

In Chung-king I met one of those missionaries — an American, by the way, who find it their chief delight to deplore the crass ignorance and presumption of people who write books on China, — or any other country, he might have added.

These worthy people assume an air of blissful modesty, and having carefully cleared the ground by asking the ignorant griffin whether he has ever written a book, blandly advise him to be quick and do it before he becomes aware of his own colossal ignorance of things Chinese.

They have of course attained the summit of that proud pinnacle themselves, and from the glorious position of monarch of all they survey, indulge in pleasantries about the people down below, who certainly cannot see everything but, from their firmer ground, can see some things with tolerable distinctness.

They never write themselves — they know too little, as they proudly inform you; and they deprecate the idea that anyone else, even more incompetent of course, should step into the breach and give to a select circle in the world a few of those gems which they themselves have so unkindly refused to impart.

Their unexpressed opinion is perhaps that fools step in where angels fear to tread; but it is a pity that they do not apply to their speech the same rule which they apply to their writings, and recognise the strict limitations of ignorance.

This missionary was of the opinion that only one book on China worth reading had ever been written; but of course he had not seen this one then.

On 3rd September we were ready to continue our voyage. Unfortunately we had just missed the steam-boat which is now running so successfully between I-chang and Chung-king, making the down trip in two days, the up trip in five, as against some six or eight weeks required to perform the same journey in the old style; but we had no difficulty in chartering a small wu-pan manned by five men, a boat which we regarded as both safer and quicker than the great clumsy junks which also make the trip through the gorges.

Having stowed our kit away in the morning, we got abroad in the afternoon and dropped down a few miles as far as the Customs hulk where we tied up for the night, spending what was to us quite a riotous evening with the officer in charge.

During the next three days we covered over three hundred miles, passing through small rapids and gorges the whole time.

High ranges of mountains rose on every hand, and the air was filled with the roar of cataracts and spinning whirlpools; the river, sometimes broad and agitated, sometimes slinking along quietly, still and and deep, between closely investing hills, seemed to be gathering itself for a spring. Whether calm and sedate or frolicking madly over the rocks, it was plainly working itself up for something better than we had yet seen.

Sunset behind us over this wonderful river was always a blaze of colour, but we were speeding away from it even while it beckoned us back to the wild west; night with its moon-lit sky filled the gorge with rippling silver which danced over the gurgling water. So we drifted on past cities and mountains, past island temples and lovely pagodas, past orange groves and many a copse and spinney, dashing through rapids, whirling helplessly round in the big racing eddies which burst around and beneath us with the roar of approaching thunder: till early on 7th September we reached K'wei-chow-fu on the borders of Szechwan and Hupei, and saw before us the cliffs of Bellows Gorge towering to the sky, and the dark slit into which the river plunged.

Suddenly the sun was hidden behind the mountain peaks,

a blast of cool air whistled out of the ragged rent in front of us, and we sped between vast cliffs rising over three thousand feet on either hand; we seemed to be speeding to some dreadful destruction, in the dark bowls of the earth. There were no rapids now. The confined water boiled and writhed around us; huge whirls sprang into existence everywhere with the crash of the avalanche, and we were at the mercy of the river, broadside on, stern first, flying round and round, while the lao-pan stood at the tiller yelling at the four oarsmen who stood on the forward deck, rowing like men demented to keep the boat's head straight wherever possible.

Presently the well-known chorus of junk-men singing at the sweeps floated up to us, followed by much shouting; so I took my camera and crawled aft to peep over the mat roof at the scenery. And what I saw almost took my breath away.

We were broadside on to the current, the river perhaps seventy-five yards in breadth.

Straight above us towered the bows of an immense junk, like a Spanish galleon, and a vast spread of white sail, bellying to the breeze, rose out of sight, completely shutting out the view. On her deck were a score of men working the big bow sweep, singing the while.

The water was creaming and frothing under her bows as she swept up under full sail, against the racing current and she was bearing right down on us, twenty yards distant, fifteen yards distant, now only ten. We were both right under the shadow of the precipice.

"Hold tight"! I said, in a voice which the sudden excitement made strained and tense; "There's going to be a collision"! Tennyson's lines —

> Thousand of their soldiers looked down from their
> decks and laughed,

> Thousands of their seamen made mock at the mad
> little craft —

seemed peculiarly appropriate to the circumstances.

But now there arose much yelling, for the great junk was on top of us.

The lao-pan screamed, the crew rowed desperately. Just as the crash seemed imminent, inevitable, the junk yawed, and swung out; there came a bump which rattled everything on board, waves dashed over our gunwale, and when we looked out, there was the junk away up the gorge, the sun glistening on her white canvas, the crew yo-ho-ing at the sweep. She had missed us by a hair's breadth, but had rocked against our stern and broken the protecting spar lashed along our side.

This was the only incident bordering on excitement during the five hundred mile trip through the rapids and gorges. Frequently a great fountain of water welled suddenly up beneath our keel, and as we spun round quite out of control, it seemed that we must be flung, helpless, against the rocks; sometimes we shave a promontory, or shoot through great tossing waves which leap over our dash-boards, swamping the forward deck. But our small boat is skilfully managed, and we come through scatheless.

Red life-boats, like large sampans, are moored at every dangerous spot, ready to shoot out from their coves to the rescue of any unfortunate victim, but we do not require their aid nor do we pass any wrecks though there are any number of boats crawling up, or sometimes humming along with the up-river breeze, under full sail, quite as fast as we are travelling down with the current.

The scenery is certainly fine, but it leaves us disappointed. Perhaps we had expected too much.

True, we had never seen a river the like of this confined between such colossal cliffs, yet we had seen bigger rapids in unnavigable rivers, higher cliffs in mountain gorges, vaster ranges in the far west.

The Yang-tse gorges appeal more to the imagination than directly to the senses of sight and sound. It is this combination of Homeric types, the immensity of the river so suddenly muzzled its unfathomed depth, the vast volume of water pouring through, the extraordinary stresses and strains set up in the compressed liquid mass, as shown by the heaving and twisting of the water, and the currents pouring in gigantic floods this way and that, up and down, that make it so unique.

A glorious day, 8th September. In the afternoon we came through the delightful Ichang gorge with its great limestone cliffs spotted with masses of vegetation shimmering in the sun, and debouched suddenly on to the dead level plain, expansive and seemingly limitless. The river broadened out, and there lay Ichang with its steamers and its bund. A thousand miles down this broad winding river was the ocean.

There was no need to delay, and we left Ichang the same night. What need to describe the luxury of a bath twice a day, or the delights of regular meals and enough to eat!

On the morning of the second day we reached the parting of the ways, Wu-chang, Han-yan, and Hankow, and there was the Han river up which we had sailed more than eleven months ago, its mouth scarcely visible amongst the forest of masts.

Then came the magnificent bund with its long line of steamers, factory chimneys, railway trains, and the clank and roar of industry.

How strange it all looked!

The day was spent ashore with friends, and in the evening we came aboard ship again, and the last stage of our journey was begun.

The rest is soon told.

Kiukiang, Wuhu, and An-king were passed on 11th September, the hottest day we had yet experienced; and Kiukiang has the reputation of being the hottest port on the river.

Next day it had cooled off considerably, and we put in to Nanking in the morning and Ching-kiang in the evening, and as we steamed away from the latter port I realised that the long journey was really over; next morning we were due to arrive in Shanghai.

That night I could not repress a feeling of excitement at the thought of meeting my friends again, and seeing the city which, though I did not love it, was after all a familiar and homelike place in China,

So we came into Woosung where the liners and men-of-war were at anchor and turned into the muddy Whang-poo, watching the old familiar scenes coming into view as we ploughed our way onwards; the miles of wharves, ships of every nation, smoking factory chimneys, and last of all the big buildings behind the trees lining the Bund.

At mid-day on 13th September we were alongside the wharf; a year all but seventeen days had passed since I sailed from Shanghai, and it had seemed half a lifetime.

A tram roared down the Bund with a horrid clanging of bells and screeching of wheels, and suddenly with the sound the terrible loneliness of a big city came upon me with full force.

Forgotten were the hardship of travel in the interior; desperately cold, hungry, tired we might have been; almost broken in spirit too sometimes, our hearts aching for a sight of civilization

But lonely — never!

And it was all forgotten now, the deadly cold that made sleep impossible, the long marches through snow and rain and burning sun, the weary climbs, the lack of food, the torturing heat of the plains with its attendant discomforts of insect life.

I only remembered the sights and cities I had seen, the mountains of ever-lasting snow, the wonderful flowers and birds, and the friends I had made.

And now it was time to say good-bye to my companion, Dr. Smith. Would I ever travel across China with him again, I wondered?

Already he had made arrangements to return to the interior within a month, big-game shooting, and had I been able, I would have accompanied him. However it was not to be.

But the grand solitude of the mountains out beyond the civilization of China is ever calling to me to return. Some day perhaps the voice will become too insistent to ignore, and I shall find myself again a willing pilgrim on the road to Tibet.

ON THE ROAD TO TIBET

About The Author

Frank Kingdon-Ward, born in Manchester in 1885, was a botanist, explorer, plant collector and author. On the Road to Tibet was the first of many books he published. He discovered and documented many plants, especially in the eastern Himalayas. He died in England in 1958.

www.ingramcontent.com/pod-product-compliance
Lightning Source LLC
LaVergne TN
LVHW030322070526
838199LV00069B/6524